This book should prove valuable in relieving stress and anxiety, especially important nowadays as the journey from diagnosis to cure or death is longer due to improvements in medical treatments. Healthcare workers and the general public worldwide would benefit from this book as death is universal. The writing style is engaging and easy to read, yet highly informative. I would recommend it to my patients and their families and friends.

Dr. Suzanne Ward, BMED, FRACGP
General Medical Practitioner
Canberra, Australia

A must read.

E. Anne Jack R.G.N. S.C.M.
Registered Nurse and Midwife (ret)
Edinburgh, Scotland, UK

The Author provides helpful, practical suggestions and has empathy with these issues.

Pat Nardone
RN with 40 Years Experience
Northern California, USA

This is an important resource for a large, needy population: a very useful guide for those facing serious disease that requires long term treatment. Carolyn is intuitive and experienced in these issues and provides excellent coverage of the topic in an easy to read format. I would have found it useful when I was in medical practice before retiring.

Richard Gracer, MD, DABFM, DABAM
Family Medicine and Pain Management Specialist
California, USA

Carolyn is a caring, professional nurse and teacher who shares clear tools and helpful ideas for people at all levels, deepening their understanding life, living, dying and death.

Sharon Sherrard
Founder of 'A Center for Inner Peace'
Instructor of 'A Course in Miracles'
Northern California, USA

A book whose time has come.

Michael C. Blank, R.N.
Registered Nurse
California, USA

After a Life-Threatening Diagnosis...What's Next...?

After a Life-Threatening Diagnosis... What's Next...?

A New Approach to Improve Healing Potential, Communications and Life Quality

Carolyn Hornblow, R.N., R.G.N. (Retired)

Routledge
Taylor & Francis Group
A PRODUCTIVITY PRESS BOOK

First Edition published 2022
by Routledge
600 Broken Sound Parkway #300, Boca Raton FL, 33487

and by Routledge
2 Park Square, Milton Park, Abingdon, Oxon, OX14 4RN

Routledge is an imprint of the Taylor & Francis Group, an informa business

Library of Congress Cataloging-in-Publication Data
A catalog record for this title has been requested

ISBN: 978-0-367-77358-8 (hbk)
ISBN: 978-0-367-77356-4 (pbk)
ISBN: 978-1-003-17098-3 (ebk)

Typeset in Garamond
by KnowledgeWorks Global Ltd.

Dedication

To my very dear friend, Michael C. Blank, R.N., without whose support and reassurance this book would never have been written. With many thanks to The Council of Twelve for the inspiration that started this journey.

Contents

Acknowledgements

I would like to thank my friends and associates for their support, assistance and encouragement. My special thanks to Betsy Glincher, Ron Ludwig, Penny Nann and David Mabbs for computer lessons and feedback. To Richard Gracer, M.D., Suzanne Ward, M.D, Pat Nardone, R.N., Sharon Sherrard and others for their book reviews and statements. To David S. Harvey, Sylvia Krug-Calder and David Cattrall for help with the book title. To Simon Pain, Specialist in Health and Safety, who connected me with my publishers. An extra special thank you to Georgie Mabbs who proofread the book and has helped me in so many ways.

Acknowledgements

About the Author

Carolyn Hornblow, RN, RGN (Retired) trained as a registered nurse and midwife in Edinburgh, Scotland, in the 1970s, where she won the Surgical Nursing Award at the Royal Infirmary of Edinburgh, UK, in 1975.

Carolyn worked internationally, in Sydney, Australia, and California, USA, for over 25 years in various nursing specialties. She qualified as an Intensive Care Specialist Nurse in Sydney, Australia in 1979.

Carolyn was involved with ladies who had breast cancer and were having breast reconstruction surgery while undergoing cancer treatment during the 1990s.

She was on the Patient Spiritual Care Committee and the Bereavement Committee at the local Scottish (NHS) hospital for a few years.

Carolyn has always had an interest in spirituality, different religious beliefs and complementary health therapies. She trained in Reiki, Therapeutic Touch and Spiritual Healing in the United States and the United Kingdom.

Ms. Hornblow recently retired, having run a successful complementary therapies clinic for the last 15 years. She was inspired to write this book over a three-week period, mostly in the early mornings. She decided to get this book published now because of the loss and distress caused by the coronavirus/COVID-19 pandemic.

Introduction: Facing Your Fears to Help You Heal

A New Approach to Survivng a Life-Threatening Illness

Firstly, I would like to welcome you to read this book! The very fact you have opened this, means you have an interest in your life and living; or that of your family and friends.

Stress, fears and anxieties can have a negative effect on your immune system and compromise healing. Traditionally, health professionals discourage you from discussing your fears as this is thought of as 'being negative'. They will tell you, 'Not to worry, there is a 90% recovery rate'. You, being human, will worry that you might be in the remaining 10%. Once diagnosed as 'terminal', then palliative care and hospice professionals do an excellent job at discussing your fears.

With cancer, the time period from diagnosis to result can be months or several years. Other medical conditions may also impact you for the rest of your life. By talking about the possibility of not surviving this illness and addressing the fears

soon after diagnosis, stress can be reduced. With less fear 'hanging over you', by feeling more in control, healing can be optimised.

We consider various complementary health therapies. Healing of the whole person (body-mind-spirit) can be integrated into your care package alongside traditional medical methods.

By looking at how you live, you can make informed choices and may decide to live life more fully now.

I was inspired to write this book over a three-week period, waking early morning, for the following main themes:

- Why releasing some of your fears may help to optimise your healing potential
- Various types of healing methods that you can do yourself at home
- Various complementary therapies which you can do while you are undergoing traditional medical treatment; optimising healing
- Suggestions on your future ideas, plans and possibilities
- Practical 'to-do' suggestions to help you organise your life, such as making a will, advanced directive/living will, estate planning, funeral choices; letting your health care and other wishes be known, even from an early age
- Ideas for how to make your 'everyday' more positive, which in turn can improve your contentment and quality of life
- Suggestions and ideas for relatives and friends coping during and after your illness, whether you actually die from this illness or much later in life
- Encouraging medical and nursing professionals to discuss your fears with you soon after diagnosis: Traditionally, this is seen as being negative and not encouraged until you are diagnosed as terminal. Rather than seen as 'being negative', this can help reduce stress and maximise your healing potential.

All these areas will help to increase your knowledge. You will feel more informed and in control in the midst of the 'storm'. By you being proactive and by expressing fears, stress levels can be reduced leading to improved healing potential.

Don't wait for the future to love your life. Don't put off until tomorrow what you can do today. Learn ways in which you can improve your contentment with who you are and how you are living right now and into the future.

WELCOME TO THE REST OF YOUR LIFE!!

Chapter 1

'I Am Sorry to Have to Tell You...'

'Your results are back and I am sorry to have to tell you but you have...'

These few words have just changed your world, your reality of who you are and your essence of being.

As the doctor continues speaking, you realise you are not really hearing the details, you are trying to 'appear normal, fine and business as usual', while you are actually in shock.

The dreaded cancer word has been spoken which might lead to dying sooner than you assumed. Or a life-shortening illness such as a heart attack, stroke, Parkinson's, motor neurone disease/ALS, also known as Lou Gehrig's disease in the United States, named after a famous baseball player there who had it.

Some of your first thoughts are likely to be 'Am I going to die from this or will I survive?' 'I'm not ready to die', 'Why me?'

These are normal human reactions to being given a diagnosis that might shorten your life.

You wonder what treatments you will have to undergo. Drugs, surgery, chemotherapy, radiotherapy?

If we are lucky, at the time of diagnosis, we are asked 'Do you have any questions?' The patient at this time tends to be so overwhelmed by the information he or she has just heard that they don't know where to begin. Hopefully, they will be able to ask the questions they have as the numbness of shock wears off.

'What should I ask?' 'I don't know the questions to ask.' 'Will I survive this?' 'Will this kill me?'

Healthcare providers, family, friends, co-workers will tend to try to minimise the impact of the news by giving positive messages of support.

Death is a stranger to us, as families have drifted apart, and grannies and grandpas are put into nursing homes to die. In Western society, we are currently disinclined to talk about death and the possibilities of dying. So death, being a stranger, becomes unknown and fearful. Yet we are all going to die, so why don't we discuss it more? Most people don't think or talk about death until *they* are the one facing it. We tend not to talk about death and not let the patient talk about it because we don't know how to respond.

This is because people do not know what to say and do not want to say the wrong thing. They put on their 'happy face', saying 'Everything is going to be just fine'. 'Don't you worry about a thing, just get better', 'The doctor knows what he/she is doing and says there is a 90% survival rate, so you'll be fine, stop worrying'.

Or else they simply don't say anything, avoiding the subject altogether as if nothing is different. As if by not talking about it, 'IT' will go away.

There is an old saying, 'If you can't say anything nice, don't say anything at all'.

I know plenty of cases where the person is faced with a life-threatening illness and, if it is a man, his male friends will call him up (if they even do that) and will banter and tell jokes, not saying how they really feel. They feel awkward and so the person is not given the space to say how they feel. Even women will be diffident about talking about 'IT'. We like to act as if it will not happen, and we tend to brush under the carpet the negative, scary thoughts. We encourage the patient, whether it is client, friend, co-worker or a family member that they will be alright, that they will get well. We discourage talk about death, labelling doubts as 'negative thinking'.

'You'll be fine, don't think about it', People say these things because they mean well; however, for the person facing the possibility of death in the near future, their need is not being addressed.

Patients often say how they felt 'abandoned' by their friends and family, not being able to talk about their fears. This was either because the patient was afraid to bring up the subject, or because they might be viewed as being scared, negative, morbid or pessimistic and they want to appear 'strong' to their loved ones and not worry them unduly. If they did bring up the subject of their possible dying, the person with them did not give them the 'space' or time to continue discussion, minimising their fears. Family and friends mean well, but they don't feel comfortable talking about death and they want to be cheerful around their loved one. So there is built a silent agreement that says 'Let's not talk about "IT"'.

By not talking about it, people think somehow it won't come to pass, that death will be avoided. There is an unconscious belief that to talk about death encourages death to come sooner.

People assume that if we don't talk about the possibility of not recovering, of dying and death, then the sufferer won't worry. Actually, the opposite is true.

We may be told 'There is a 90% cure rate so you'll be fine, your chances are very good', but we will tend to think 'Yes, but what about that 10% fail rate, what if I am in that 10% group?'

We naturally tend to give ourselves a lot of negative self-talk. That is just human nature.

We are programmed to focus and hear the negative rather than the positive. A research study of children in a European Kindergarten was undertaken. It was discovered that the children were given two or three negative comments, 'No, stop, bad, wrong, naughty', in comparison to positive comments.

Think about the stock market reports. If it goes up fifty points, what degree of attention do you put on that versus if it falls fifty points?

When I got my school report if I had four A grades and two B grades my father would ask, 'Why did you only get four A's? Next time I want to see all A's'...so it was never enough and my pride/self-esteem was crushed.

The news is full of the negative. If it were positive, how many of us would stop to listen, or change channels to get more information? Yet that is what a lot of us do. We are much more used to negative words such as, 'don't', 'no', 'can't', than positive, 'yes', 'good', 'well done'.

We do tend as human beings to focus on the negative more than the positive. We often have to remind ourselves to focus on the 'good' things that are in our lives and not just take them for granted.

Think about this, at the end of a busy day, you have probably been told a few times 'thanks for your help', 'you do a great job', and you have been given one negative comment. I'll bet that you spent 90% of your time that evening focusing on the one negative comment and not even 10% on all the positive comments you have received.

In some cases, you were not even aware that you were even given a positive comment; you may not even consciously have heard it. This is a very common thing that we all do – we focus on the criticism and we fail to hear the praise, or we minimise it, brushing it aside.

As People We Focus on the Negative!

So with that knowledge, imagine being told by the doctor that you have cancer and the kind that you have is 90% curable. Where do you think your attention is going to go and what would you obsess and worry over?

That's right…the 10% that do not recover and are not curable! People will say to you 'Don't worry, there is a 90% cure rate, your chances are very good'. Yet all through the diagnosis time, possible surgery, chemotherapy and radiation, you are wondering and worrying about 'Am I going to be one of the 90% or one of the 10%?'

If you are like most people, you will find yourself thinking about the 10% failure rate for larger part of the time during your treatments, which can take months or years. During the whole process, you probably lie in bed at night, worrying about the 'what ifs'.

As a patient with cancer told me, 'You go to bed and the last thing you think about is your cancer, and it is the first thing you think about when you wake in the morning. It hangs over your head like a noose'.

'Please let me live another day…until my child grows up… until my grandchild is born'. These thoughts and prayers are repeated frequently at the assessment time, surgery, chemotherapy, radiation and time awaiting the final result. 'Am I cured or will this kill me?'

Only when the doctor tells you that you are cured, which can be months or years after the initial diagnosis, will you breathe a sigh of relief. You hope you won't get a reoccurrence and maybe only then admit to your friends and family how worried you were. They will tend to admit that they were also terribly worried, but, 'Did not want to upset you or worry you, especially as you seemed to be handling it so well'.

How much easier, better and less stressful it would have been to openly discuss these concerns and worries right up front, at the beginning, shortly after the initial diagnosis. By doing so, how much easier and less stressful would the journey have been?

If the people you shared these concerns with were able to give you the support, space, freedom and encouragement to talk about your fears, you would have felt supported and freer to be the 'real' you, not the 'public' you.

I firmly believe that by being open, honest and encouraging the person to talk about the 'what ifs' of possible death from the disease and the fears that accompany this, early on after the diagnosis, we can help the person reduce their fears and stress, and promote an optimum, psychological and physical basis with which to fight the disease.

If 90% of the patient's focus is on the negative, fearful worry area, then only 10% is available for the positive, healing focus.

By changing these percentages, even a little bit, there will be more positive energy available for promoting healing.

Maybe the percentage of worry time and negative can be brought down from 90% to 50%. The extra energy that is released from the continual negative undercurrent of worry and fear, of '*what if I die, what will happen to me after I die, and what is dying like?*', can instead be converted into positive energy to help promote the chances of healing.

I believe that by giving the patient information, allowing discussion and encouraging them to openly talk about their fears helps the patient feel less frightened. By diminishing some of the fears and anxiety, we empower the patient and they feel less stressed.

By breaking the stress cycle early on in therapy, we can help the patient reduce their fear response, easing their course of treatment and promoting the chances of healing and recovery. No one heals well if stressed. Not all the stress, fear and anxiety can be removed but it can be reduced.

You cannot change the Past,
but you can change the Present
To have an impact on your Future!

Chapter 2

Facing the Fear – To Help You Heal

Life is precious and short – and whether you die aged 10 or 99, life is too short until *you* are ready to die! And are any of us ready, ever, to die? Wouldn't you take any opportunity possible to increase your chances of full recovery? You really have just two choices with a life-threatening diagnosis – Fight it or let it kill you without a battle.

When you have a disease that is threatening your life you tend to feel powerless, overwhelmed and frightened, especially initially, when there is so much to find out about.

What kind of cancer do you have, or other type of potentially life-shortening illness? What are the types of treatments and options? How sick the illness or treatments will make you? Will surgery make you disfigured? Can you still work during treatment?

There are so many questions to be asked and answered about your disease, treatment options and factors that will affect you. By gaining information, you can help yourself feel less scared and anxious and more in control. By talking about the scared part of you, some of the degree of fear will lessen.

By facing the 'death dragon' as I like to label the situation, or 'DD' for short, we can realise that it is not quite SO scary.

An analogy I like to use is the child who goes to bed scared that there is something under the bed that is going to 'get them'. As the child lies in his/her dark room thinking about the monster under the bed, the monster becomes bigger and bigger. The child doesn't dare get out of the bed to go to the bathroom, as they are convinced that as soon as they put a foot over the side of the bed, they will be swallowed by the monsters, because now there are at least two! They have not told their parents that this fear is constant because they don't want their parents to know that they are scared. This goes on nightly, as the child gets into bed and tries to fall asleep. As long as the room is dark, the fears about the monster grow and become more real and scary. If the child puts on the bedside light and looks under the bed (if they even dare), they find there is actually nothing there. But as soon as the light goes out, the monster is back, ready to get them! You may laugh at this, but when I was seven or eight, I would search my room before getting into bed. I'd look in the cupboard, behind the chest of drawers and under the bed at least once nightly to try to reassure myself that there were no monsters. But as soon as the light went out, I KNEW that the monster lurked under my bed and only when the light was on, or if I stayed in bed, was I safe.

The imagination of the fearful child builds and builds and the monster under the bed grows, causing the child to focus more and more attention on the fears and the 'what ifs'. We, as adults, are no different; we are essentially the same child, only bigger!

I liken this to the person facing the possibility of dying. By not giving them the freedom to discuss their fears, we keep them from being able to turn the light on their fears, and that fear becomes their own monster, the 'DD'. They lie in bed at night with fears running through their minds, worries getting bigger and bigger, the monster growing.

If we face the monster in the shadows, and speak about it and ask it to come into the light, or 'turn the light on it', we can see that it is not as big and scary as it seems when allowed to dwell in the darkness of unacknowledged fears.

By 'turning on the light' of expression and discussion, these fears can be talked about and the worry and distress be eased.

When the patient is ready, by allowing ourselves to discuss perfectly normal fears, we are not encouraging death or accepting it. We are getting to know about the possibilities we are facing and getting to know the facts as much as we can. By doing so we reduce the amount of fear, and reduce the size of the 'DD'.

So, by shedding light into the dark recess of the mind, we can be less stressed about the 'what ifs' of dying. This does not mean you are being negative, morbid or giving up and not fighting the disease. It is simply becoming as informed as you can be, by looking at death and what possibly happens beyond, as best we know. I encourage you to explore various religious beliefs, read books on reincarnation and near-death experiences (NDE) and think about what is important to you.

By looking at the possibility of dying, it makes us take hold of living in the present!

Traditionally, doctors and nurses tend to not encourage talk of dying or 'not making it'. It is viewed as being negative and is often discouraged. So, often the opportunity to allow the patient to discuss their fears are negated. I once asked a registered nurse in charge of the chemotherapy department at the hospital I worked in, where patients regularly came for hours, frequently, for treatment, whether she allowed her patients to express their fears? She was shocked and said, 'Good Heavens, I don't allow anything like that in my clinics; that is far too negative!' What a missed opportunity, and I think this would not happen if they were aware of the positivity of patients expressing their questions and fears.

Negative, personal and intimate thoughts tend not to be discussed openly, unless talking to a counsellor. 'People want or need to appear 'upbeat' – successful, positive thinking – and they tend to feel that dwelling on death and dying or to talk about it is negative or weak. We need to be able to say to people, 'It is alright to be frightened, talk with me about your fears. Get them out into the open so we can face them, look at them and hopefully lessen them'.

The personnel involved in palliative care and hospice care, once known as terminal care, are comfortable at letting patients discuss their fears.

We Should Not Wait until Diagnosed as Terminal

'A problem shared is a problem halved' is an old saying but a wise one. I know that when I talk to my friends and share my worries and concerns over issues that are troubling me, I feel that the degree of burden is lightened.

Removing some of the stressful negative fears allows that percentage of energy to be converted into positive energy for improving your chances of healing. We all know that there is a lot of stress around. We need some stress to get us out of bed in the mornings, to 'get on with the day'. Problems occur when stress is maintained, when there is no ability to fight or flee from the stressors. Many support groups have a 24-hour helpline or advice nurses during normal working hours. Also, there are online groups for support amongst fellow patients.

Being given a diagnosis of a potentially life-threatening illness is one of the biggest stressors that I can think of and you can't run away from it – as it is inside you!

On top of that, you are facing drugs, chemotherapy, radiation and possibly surgery. More stress and fear about events coming up. With the various medical interventions and treatments there is anticipated and real discomfort and pain!

Pain, nausea and other discomforts can be taken care of with various medications. However, studies show that healing occurs more slowly when the patient is stressed or in pain.

Stress can build on itself and affect the human body and mind negatively and has a huge impact on our ability to cope. **Stress and fear increase perceived pain levels**. However, if stress can be reduced then the degree of pain and discomfort can be diminished and pain medication may be able to be lessened.

The ability to reduce some of the stress and thereby lower pain levels, or increase the tolerance of pain, is a significant factor, as pain can be its own monster. You can be in a room, in pain, and the nurses are busy, or it is 'not time' for your pain medication. You are wrapped up in the pain and can think of nothing else.

This happened to me after knee surgery. I was not facing a life-threatening illness, just a simple post-operative situation, experiencing pain. I felt out of control because I was 'trapped' in the bed with a knee splint and unable to get pain medication because it was not 'time'. The nurses were busy and despite my using the call bell, no one was coming in to check out what the problem was.

I felt engulfed in my pain and I felt 'wrong' because I was told I 'should not be feeling this degree of pain at this stage'. I was fearful, stressed and my pain was increasing. I felt totally out of control and was crying. It took just one nurse to make the difference. He came into the room, sat beside me and assured me that all I needed to do was ask, and if the pain medication did not help me, he would call my doctor to increase the dosage order. I felt like a weight was lifted off my shoulders. I felt that I was being listened to and being allowed to be in control. This was a proactive way of dealing with my pain. I remember him like an angel in the middle of my own personal hell of pain. My pain medication was effective, I slept well and never had to call him again during the night. This was an episode that happened to me 30 years ago and I still can remember the feeling of being out of control, caught up in my pain. He made such a difference to my experience.

The use of patient-controlled analgesia (PCA) machines can also provide a similar feeling of control. PCA machines deliver a dose of pain medication to the patient through an intravenous line, when the patient pushes a button. There is a preset limit to how much medication the patient can get. The scientific concern was that patients would abuse and overuse the medication and that it should be restricted. However, the findings are that when the patient has the choice and control of when to use the medication, the usage is actually reduced. When the patient is made not to depend on someone else to provide relief and knows he/she can push the button whenever needed, then the amount of medication is significantly reduced. Why? Because the patient has control and the stress and fear of anxiety around the 'what ifs' of being in pain and not being able to get the pain medication are gone. You cannot overdose because there is a limit set.

Control and empowerment = Reduced stress = Reduced pain!!

When in pain you feel scared, alone and distressed, out of pain you feel more relaxed and healing can take place. When someone takes a little time to stop and connect with you, you also feel better, and less alone.

You can be in a crowded room full of people and feel totally alone, the wallflower, the misfit. Having people around you doesn't stop you from feeling alone. One person can make a difference and by reaching out and asking someone 'Can I help you? How are you doing? Is there anything you want to talk about?' can make such a difference.

ALONE   ADD AN 'L' (FOR LOVE/KINDNESS) = ALL ONE

This table is just an outline of how the stress cycle can affect us. The order is variable, and not all symptoms are experienced by everyone.

The Stress Cycle

Diagnosis = Am I going to die from this? = FEAR and SHOCK
Increased anxiety = disease present, facing surgery chemotherapy, radiation
Increased fight or flight response = increased sustained stress
Increased adrenaline levels
Increased heart rate, increased blood pressure
Increased pain and restlessness
Poor sleep pattern/wakefulness
Nightmares
Mood alteration = anxiety/depression/irritability
Poor appetite
Increased perception of pain and disease
Decreased communication
Withdrawal
Increased feelings of aloneness
Decreased standard of well-being
Diminished immune system strength

It is a vicious cycle that we can get into, similar to that of a mouse on a circular tread wheel, going around and around. It feeds on itself, getting deeper and deeper. The person can try to stop it cycling down, but it can be hard work.

Talking about your fears can reduce some of the negative stress. It probably will not take all of it away, but it does release a degree of stress which in turn can be converted into a more positive mental and physical state which in turn promotes healing potential.

Breaking the Stress Cycle

- Informed patient, fears expressed = LESS FEAR
- Decreased fight/flight response
- Lower adrenaline levels
- Decreased restlessness/anxiety
- Less stress
- Lower heart rate
- Lower blood pressure
- Improved sleep
- More rested
- Calmer mental outlook
- Higher pain threshold so more able to tolerate pain
- Better appetite
- Improved communication
- Improved level of well-being
- Improved immune system response

Being given permission by family, friends and the doctors and nurses to openly talk about your fears will help minimise them, or at least help to reduce them when they arise from time to time, which they are bound to do. This, in turn, will help reduce the stress cycle or prevent it from building up, and it will be easier for you to remain more relaxed and less worried.

This will help your body's ability to heal, from surgery, chemotherapy, radiation and the illness itself.

We, as human beings, heal quicker when at rest and not stressed, mentally as well as physically.

Recovery, hopefully, will be speedier and chances of metastasis or progression of disease diminished.

When antibiotics were not yet invented, tuberculosis (TB) cures were achieved in sanatoriums by the patient resting, relaxing and getting exposure to sunshine.

Nowadays, we call that recipe a holiday or stress reduction!

Reduction of stress is known scientifically to be beneficial to healing and wellness, so anything that helps reduce stress, spoken or unspoken, must be of benefit for the person trying to get well. Being less stressed makes it easier for us to cope with any issue.

By expressing the fears *early on* after diagnosis and discuss, explore and face the possibility of death in the early phase of treatment, reduces stress. This in turn can increase the potential for healing at the beginning of the battle, shortly after being given a life threatening diagnosis.

Chapter 3

Knowledge about Dying Reduces Stress

We are all going to die at some point, so it would be good to be a little informed.

Death is a strange affair and depending on who you are, where you live and what your religious beliefs are, your demise will either be celebrated or mourned.

People will wear white or black clothes. There will be sombre funerals or lively parties. You will be buried below or above ground or you may be burned in a crematorium or floated out to sea!

Wherever you are, there will be a different way of marking your death.

Hushed whispers, window blinds pulled down, wearing black for a year, black armbands, mourning brooches, or party time and celebrations that you have completed your life and are now continuing on your spiritual path.

When my father died, my uncle, on his arrival for the funeral asked me in hushed tones, 'Is it OK to talk about your Dad?' As if, now he was dead, he could not be talked about!

In the Western world, we celebrate birth and marriage. There are celebratory parties, gifts given, photos taken. What do we do with death and dying? We talk in lowered tones about death, we don't even like saying the word. We wear dark clothing and try to move away from the experience as soon as possible; we feel uncomfortable about death.

We need to be able to come to a point of celebrating a person's life and realise that they have moved on to another level of existence. Life is a journey of experience and learning, and then we die.

Yes, we shall miss them and grieve for their absence, but if a person has had a good life and a fulfilled one, celebrate that, and remember the laughs and the good times. Realise that, as we are taught in churches and religious places, the person has moved on to a far, far better place.

In many places and with many people, there is a fear of talking about cancer, for fear it might be catching and result in death. Even the word 'cancer' was not spoken, or if it was, it was referred to as the 'Big C'. Better not to talk about 'IT'. 'Don't tempt fate!'

We must try to get through this layer of fear around death.

Reading about dying peoples' experiences, past-life regressions and near-death experiences (NDEs) will help us gain more awareness and understanding.

Hopefully, we can get to the point of celebrating death as we celebrate life.

Once we are born into this life and are alive in this physical body, death is inevitable. There is no escaping it; it is just a question of when!

Let us learn about it so we can lead rich fulfilling lives and not be fearful of the ending.

Why do we send young people off to war and why is it that usually it is the young who do the death-defying acts of dangerous sports, car racing etc.? Because they do not fear death, not yet.

As they get older and wiser, and life gives them a few knocks, they start to realise that they are not all-knowing and immortal. Their life becomes more precious to them and the risks they are prepared to take reduce. So they gradually stop being risk-takers and thrill-seekers.

'I won't do that…it might be dangerous, I don't want to run the risk.'

As people mature, they are less willing to defy death and sometimes fear of death immobilises their actions.

If we learned more about death and if it was talked about, I believe we would learn to accept it as a fact of life. We would free ourselves up to lead enriching fulfilling lives and not be fearful of change so much, including our inevitable ending of physical life. I am not saying let's accept death blindly. I *am* saying let's talk about it, discuss fears and beliefs and by doing so, reduce the level of fear we all have of the 'unknown'.

Death is viewed by many in different ways. In the Tarot, card 13 is the 'death card' and is often depicted with a skeleton or scythe. When people first see it in their played hand, they immediately think it means death. In fact its interpretation is that of transition, of clearing away the old to allow new things to come into their life, a change.

Often, in order to have new things or events come into your life, you have to let go of some old things. Old belongings, a job that doesn't work for you, patterns of living that are not beneficial to you, in order to create space to allow the new to enter.

People need to get comfortable with death. Death is not a failure – it is a part of life and living. It is a stage of life.

What do you say to someone who is dying? People don't know what to say to you when they think you might be dying. Some thoughts go like this:

> Poor Joe, he doesn't look that bad.
> I don't know what to say.

> If you can't think of anything nice to say, say nothing.
> What if I say the wrong thing?
> You look great – I'm sure you'll be fine.
> Don't worry, you'll just upset yourself.
> I'm sure the doctor knows best.
> Think positive; don't be negative.
> What if I lose him/her?
> What if it is catching?
> How do I touch him/her?
> What if I hurt him/her?

Very often, people stay away from the patient, fearful of saying the wrong thing.

We are given many messages that talking about death is morbid, negative, a failure.

But by not saying anything or avoiding the issue, we tend to promote the person's feelings of isolation or being abandoned by family, friends and the medical profession.

We need to learn to communicate our love, to listen to the needs of the person and touch their heart, their Being/ Essence/Spirit/Soul/Mind – whatever you want to call it.

I had one patient who told me that after diagnosis of breast cancer, she was helped by her minister who was very caring and supportive. However, her husband was so upset by her diagnosis that he withdrew from her and wouldn't touch her. He was frightened of loss and did not know what to say or do. So he 'abandoned' her by shutting her out, due to his confusion and fear. Feeling alone, separate and uncertain of the unknown can be frightening. Yet it is something that we are all going to do. There is no written excuse for it, no optional participation, no choice. At some time, sooner or later, we will face death and 'cross the great divide' (which we possibly crossed when we were born).

Death does not have to be like that and should not be like that.

We should aim for beautiful graceful deaths. We aim for beautiful marriages, why not aim for beautiful deaths?

What do I mean by a beautiful 'good' death? Peaceful, calm acceptance, relaxed, sleeping well, eating well; feeling in control as much as possible. Any pain being managed well without unnecessary levels of drowsiness and drug-induced confusion and nausea; knowing that everything has been done medically. Their affairs in order, such as their wills, living wills, advanced directives complete. They are accepting that they are ready to progress to the next stage; knowing they have lived a happy, fulfilled life.

They have said what they wanted to say to friends and family. Friends and family have all said their goodbyes and have said what is in their hearts.

Being able to openly discuss fears, or talk about any visions or dreams or 'out of body' experiences that they are having. Relatives and loved ones who have died may be 'seen'. Some people think that they have come to take the patient 'home'.

Most people do not know and have not even seen death. It is a great mystery, kept in the dark. We even refer to death in a euphemistic fashion 'He's gone to sleep', 'He's gone to God/heaven/joined the angels'.

Maybe you are dying to talk about it...but no one will let you.

What nice things can you say about death? We don't know because we don't talk about it.

How many people visit a morgue?
How many people see dying and death?
How many people talk about or discuss death?
How many people celebrate death?
Death tends to be the great unknown until we have to face it ourselves in the final hours. The unknown is very scary and frightening which in turn increases adrenaline levels, stress and pain levels.
Death is the great unknown – True to a large degree

Death is coming to us all – True!!
Death is final – Is it??
Death is the end of life – Is it, or is it a change in the way we exist?
You cease to 'be' when you die. Do you?
What and who are you [body, mind, spirit]?
Why did you come to this planet earth in the first place?
Have you achieved what you came to do; if you even have an idea what that was?
Have you contributed to society, helped others? Or was it all about getting rich, gaining money, power, fame, etc., and has that brought you 'happiness'?

These are great questions for all of us. It makes us look at life and think, who are we, why we are here and are we achieving our aims and ambitions. Or are we just coasting along life's path or have we just given up, ceased to try, too fearful to try something different?

These are fundamental questions but we don't like to talk about death so we don't bring up the questions and yet there is a hunger for information.

When a book comes out about NDEs, it sells like hotcakes.

There are talk shows and movies on the near-death subject because people are 'dying' to find out what dying is all about!

Yet books on death and dying in a bookstore are too often tucked away under the self-help category and not clearly labelled.

There are lots of questions and lots of fear if you are the one facing 'IT'.

Yet there are very few experts sure of what to say because none of us have truly been dead and then come back to talk about it!

Am I going to die? The answer to that is a resounding yes! Unless you are the first person not to do so in the history of mankind, you are going to die at some point in the near or distant future. That is a certainty. Life and living comes to an end at some point for each and every one of us. It is inevitable, but death does not have to be a monster hiding in the shadows waiting to pounce. I encourage you to explore death; the ideas, concepts, opinions – face the demon and see what makes sense to you, what feels right to you.

What nice things can we say about death? We don't know because we don't discuss it.

I once brought the subject up at a party and got some very strange looks! My cousin's reaction when I told him what I was writing about was one of resistance initially. He responded, 'Well, I don't think that is a positive subject!'

In Medicine, it is not usually directly discussed until the patient is deemed 'terminal', at which point you are transferred to the palliative care team, who are expert at talking about death and dying. Many would like to die at home or hospice. However, approximately 50% of us will die in hospital.

My experience with death started around the age of three when I worried that my mother was going to die and leave me, because she was very ill with typhoid fever.

I had been told by someone that I had to be very good or my mummy might die – I was so good that it was abnormal!

My next lesson was suddenly, at age seven, when I was told that my favourite grandpa had gone to sleep and I could not see him again. As I had seen him asleep before and had played with him after he had awoken, I found this news puzzling, but as he never appeared again to play, I gradually accepted it.

Then, at age nine, a girl at school whom I didn't like, and whom I had not been very nice to, died suddenly. I wondered if somehow my not being nice to her had contributed to her death and I felt guilty over it.

The first time I saw death was at age thirteen, in hospital, when an elderly lady in the bed opposite me died suddenly.

The nurses rushed in and closed the curtains and took the rest of us out of the room. When we came back later, the bed was empty and no one spoke of her dying. I remember being interested that she had been struggling with breathing and coughing, and that dying had almost been a relief for her. As I was being pushed, by wheelchair out of the room, my extended foot opened her curtains briefly and she looked so peaceful and it had happened so quickly. I remember that most vividly.

Then I went into nursing and no one prepares you for the dying and how to deal with the event. We were told in nursing school just to manage as 'best we could'.

For my first 'patient death', I was taught by the auxiliary nurse; who made me touch the elderly lady as we washed her and put her body into a shroud, ready for the morgue.

I remember thinking how it was just a body, slightly stiff, heavy and difficult to move around because all 'assistance' from the person was gone.

Her essence, energy or being that had been there was gone – it was just a shell, a body remaining.

My worst experience was of a girl, in her 20s, who had shot her boyfriend. Before being arrested, she had poured petrol over her body and set herself alight, becoming a human torch. She came into the intensive care unit and there was nothing we could do. I was assigned to sit with her for the few hours she had remaining, giving her morphine and watching her die. At one point, she turned her head to me and asked, 'Am I going to die?' and I, at age 24, couldn't tell her the truth. I 'chickened out' and reassured her that she would be alright. I asked another more mature nurse to sit with her instead. I always felt that I failed her by not being truthful in the moment, but I did not know what to say. I hope that if I was asked the same question now by her, I would honour her enough to be honest with her and not let my inexperience get in the way. Her death has remained with me and I find I am unable to nurse patients with burns.

Other experiences have always left me with a respect for death. It always seems to me that if a person has been struggling with discomfort or difficulty breathing, that death is peaceful, a release, an end of pain and restlessness; I seem to see a look of peace on the person's face. The image I always have is of calm and of movement; that the essence, soul or being of the person has moved on, gone.

All that remains is the body casing or shell, like a discarded envelope. The letter or vital content, the spirit, has gone elsewhere.

Many healthcare professionals can give you stories of timings of death and how some people choose the time they will die.

The one that sticks in my mind is of a lady who was waiting for a much loved niece to arrive from a distance. It had taken the niece a few days to get to the hospital. She arrived and had some time with her aunt. Then the aunt quietly died, having stayed alive much longer than we had thought possible.

Another story is of the family who would not leave the grandfather alone and there was always someone in the room with him. After two days of this, an unexpected person showed up to visit. The family decided to go down to the cafeteria for 15 minutes and left the grandfather alone. The grandfather died in those 15 minutes. It was as if he was unable to leave his body while the family was present. As soon as they left the room, he 'left' too.

It seems to take a certain amount of energy for a person to die, for the soul to leave the body. When there are people in the room they can subconsciously hold a person back from dying by willing them to get better, by holding their hand, talking non-stop.

Both my father and grandmother died while no one was right beside them. There were people in the house but in the few minutes they had been left alone, they moved on.

My mother, both times, said she wished she had been there with them, but I think that they needed to transition and someone's presence, trying to keep them alive, can get in the way.

Let us talk about death and life and *then get on with living life to the full while we still have the gift of life.*

By talking about death, we realise that life is a gift. Not just days to get up and endure and work through, but that we have been given a precious gift of limited time. By realising this, we can go forward and live it to the best of our ability and not waste time.

Am I going to die? Yes I am, it is just a question of how and when.

So let me look at my fears around that and prepare for the inevitable. By looking at the issue, I can then review how I am living my life. Do I like that way or is there a better way for me to live for whatever time I have left? Whether it be months or years?

Let us all stop hiding our heads in the sand like ostriches. This is life. It is not a dress rehearsal, so let's get it right.

It is an event that takes place in an instant, like walking out of your front door into a different landscape. One minute you are on the physical plane, the next you are here in the spiritual realms, celebrating your life and experiences and allowing us to embrace you and welcome you home. The big event that you fear is simply nothing for your spirit to go through. It is a slipping or passing through the veil of separation between the two worlds of physical and spiritual.

'DEATH IS NOTHING AT ALL' Meditation by Canon Henry-Scott Holland Died 1918

Death is nothing at all… I have only slipped away into the next room.

I am I and you are you. Whatever we were to each other…that we still are.

Call me by my old familiar name. Speak to me in the easy way you used to
Put no difference into your tone, wear no forced air of solemnity or sorrow.
Laugh as we always laughed at the little jokes we enjoyed together.
Play, smile, think of me, pray for me.
Let my name be ever the household word that it always was.
Let it be spoken without affect, without the ghost of a shadow on it.
Life means all that it ever meant. It is the same as it ever was.
There is absolutely unbroken continuity.
What is this death but a negligible accident?
Why should I be out of mind because I am out of sight?
I am just waiting for you, for an interval, somewhere very near, just around the corner.
All is well.

We all want to fit into society and we conform by listening to the messages that society gives us, about what is acceptable, what is OK and what is not.

We are encouraged to go around with an 'I'm OK face' – 'I'm coping, I'm strong, I am fine'. Inside us, however, is the frightened part, the private part of ourselves that we find hard to show to others.

Will it be scary? Will I be alone?

We do not get to do this journey with anyone else. It is a single, one-way ticket and we are all going to do it, yet very few people are talking about 'IT'.

We are all going to die at some point in time, so let us try to do it as well as possible.

Don't let us increase our fears by not talking about death. Let us explore death a little so we can reduce our fears and worries and give ourselves a better chance for healing.

Look at your life.

Do you like how you are living, your job and your activities? Do you want to make a change and have been too afraid to do so, or become stuck in a rut?

I know of a man who was told he had one year remaining. He chose to leave his wife and move into a lady friend's house for his last year.

There is a great story about a man who saw a large table across the room from him, with everything he ever wanted to eat. In the palm of his hands were stale crisps that he was very used to; they fed him and sustained him and he was used to them. He realised he really wanted the feast, but in order to reach it, he had to let go of the crisps and walk across the room to the table of lovely food. The gap between releasing the stale crisps and walking across the room is called RISK!

Based on this story, I quit a job that was 'alright' and got a better job in a nearby town.

Do you want to make a change that might improve your journey through life or wait until you retire?

Life and death are very much intertwined. By looking at death, we throw new light on life and a possible new way of being.

By not looking at death actively, we may never shed light on our life. We always assume we will live a long time and have time to change. So we may die thinking, 'If only I'd thought about this before and not been too frightened to make changes, I could have had a more meaningful life'.

Awareness is 90% cure. Let's become aware, by looking at death, and its issues for us, square in the face. By doing so, we can choose to make powerful positive transformational changes to our lives right now. We can improve the quality of our lives, the depths of our friendship, the degree of intimacy with our loved ones and be vibrant with our lives, instead of drifting through the time we have been given.

Life is a gift we are given, to use for the benefit of ourselves and others. Earth is rather like a playground or school and our lives are the lessons. Some of the most difficult times in our lives are our greatest teachers. There are people who believe we choose our main lesson, the reason why we come here to Earth. They believe we choose our parents and situations that will best help us learn our lessons.

There is a saying that God never gives you a lesson that He feels you cannot handle. That an obstacle viewed one way can be an opportunity, if viewed in a different light.

We are possibly given a gift by getting a life-threatening illness; an opportunity to assess where we are and what we are doing with our life.

We can become 'aware' and then be creative if we choose to. We may not get the choice of when we die, in the near or distant future, but we can certainly make changes if we want to, in how we live the life we have been given, while we have it!

I believe that if we come to terms with our lives, accept the life we have or change it; then when it is our turn to die we will accept it more peacefully. We will accept with fewer struggles because we will feel that we have truly lived. Hopefully we will feel that we have accomplished what we came here to do and now are ready to return to our spiritual home.

What you are is God's gift to you...
What you do with it is your gift to God.

Chapter 4

'To Life' Fix, Cure or Heal? Going for It All

What is the difference between these focuses? Healing is making a person whole, focusing on the three levels of man: body, mind and spirit. Curing is a 'fixing' of the person, seeking a cure or remission of the physical body illness, with little or no focus on the emotional, mental and spiritual aspect of the patient.

Western medicine tends currently to focus on the fix or cure of the physical body through various means, in order to remove or kill the problem, organism or growth. There are many illnesses that can be life-threatening or life-shortening. Sometimes, it can be less than a year from the time of diagnosis to dying or it can be several years. I want to address the possible treatments that you will undergo if you have been diagnosed with cancer. I don't intend to go into this in depth as there are many books written about cancer treatments. Also, you will be well guided by your physician, surgeon and oncologist (cancer specialist). There are excellent support groups that offer help and advice for medical treatments and possible side effects as well as emotional support.

Traditional Medical Treatment

I STRONGLY ENCOURAGE YOU TO GET TO KNOW ABOUT YOUR TYPE OF CANCER AND POSSIBLE OPTIONS FOR TREATMENT. Get second or even third opinions, preferably at different hospitals so there is no professional conflict of interest. Research and ask questions. Take a notepad and pen with you to your consultations. This way you will remember the questions you wanted to ask and write down the answers. Do not be rushed or minimised.

This does have a positive effect on you and your health team. You might even want to check how other countries treat your type of cancer. There are different types of treatments and what you receive will depend very much on the kind of cancer you have, the place where it is and how advanced (big) or what 'stage' the cancer is. It is important that you let your healthcare team know if you are on any 'over-the-counter' medications from your chemist or pharmacy. Are you taking any vitamins or herbal medications or undergoing any complementary therapies?

Some treatments are used for just one area. These are called localised or local treatments and include surgery and radiotherapy. Systemic treatments are given for therapy throughout the body and may include chemotherapy, hormonal therapies, targeted therapies and immunotherapies.

Surgery

The primary aim will be to remove as much of the tumour as possible by surgery. This may be a day surgery where you spend just the day in the hospital and go home that night or you may have to stay in the hospital for one or two days. The amount of tissues removed that are surrounding the tumour will depend on the size and location of the tumour. In the case of a skin cancer such as melanoma, there will be a wide excision beyond the actual visible mole as well as being quite deep. If the lymph nodes in the groin or the armpits are involved or near the melanoma, some or all of those nodes may well be removed as well. In the case of breast cancer, it may be a decision of surgical excision of the tumour with a little bit of the skin surrounding it which would be called a lumpectomy. It is fairly uncommon nowadays to do a full breast removal which is called a mastectomy. Very often, the axillary lymph nodes in the armpit are removed and examined microscopically as well as the tumour. Sometimes, the beginnings of breast reconstruction are done at the same time as the breast tissue is removed. The tumour and the nodes are examined microscopically to see whether there is any cancer in the tumour and lymph nodes and what kind/type of cancer it is and what 'stage' has it reached. Stages are a way of defining how large the tumour is and whether it has spread. Your oncologist, who is a doctor specialising in cancer treatment, will decide what are the best treatment(s) options to eliminate any residue of cancer. It might be that nothing extra is required and that the excision of the tumour is enough. It might be that you will need a course of radiotherapy and/or a course of chemotherapy as a follow-up to the excision. In some cases, a course of radiotherapy or chemotherapy is given prior to the surgical excision.

Chemotherapy

It is not uncommon to have surgery followed up by a course of chemotherapy. Chemotherapy is a cocktail of drugs designed to eliminate any remaining cancer. What drugs are given depends on the kind and type of cancer that you have. This treatment may be oral tablets or given intravenously which means a needle is put into a vein, usually in your arm, and fluids containing the chemicals/drugs are administered over a period of time. Depending on the drug, it may be a couple of hours or it could be several hours and one drug or several drugs may be administered. This can be over a three- to four-week cycle, repeated over three to six months. Very often, this is done in a large room with other patients who are also receiving their chemotherapy. Unfortunately, some of the medications can cause hair loss. You may be offered an ice scalp cap during treatment to help reduce the hair loss and there will probably be a wig specialist who can help you with a choice of wigs. Very often when the hair regrows, if you had straight hair before, you might well find you have soft curly hair. Another unpleasant side effect can be nausea and vomiting. You will be given medication to help reduce this side effect. Tiredness (fatigue) is a common symptom during treatment. Weight changes can also occur. Some people experience a sore mouth and throat. Side effects might be mild or strong. Some may just occur during treatment and a few might persist after treatment. Finger tingling and coldness can be a persistent symptom in some cases. Everyone is an individual, so some experience no side effects. This does not mean that the treatment is not working. Discuss any symptoms with your health team. They can advise you and may change the drug you are on if symptoms become very troublesome.

Radiotherapy

Radiation therapy is a means of irradiating and eradicating a tumour using high-energy x-rays called photons. It is usually done over a series of weeks, usually five to six weeks, five days a week. The actual time you receive the treatment is brief so you can be in and out from the department after just thirty minutes. There can be preparation beforehand to make sure that the treatment is focused just on the tumour site. This may involve a facial mask being made for you to keep your head still while receiving the treatment on your face or head if that is where the tumour is. It might require a small tattoo as a marker for the beam of light, so that the exact same area is treated each time. This is a painless treatment but as the weeks proceed you can experience tiredness and your skin can get quite tender. You will be given advice as to how to take care of any skin problems you might experience.

Proton Beam Therapy

This is a targeted treatment used for certain cancers with highly specific targeting of the affected area. Especially useful for hard to reach tumours close to vital organs. Lower radiation exposure to healthy surrounding tissue.

Immunotherapy

This is a treatment to boost your own immune system, to help it identify and attack cancer cells. It is a targeted treatment to help slow or stop the growth of cancer cells or prevent them from spreading elsewhere in your body. It can be administered orally, intravenously, topically with cream onto the skin or by a catheter into the bladder. All the chemotherapy and radiotherapy treatments can result in profound tiredness for a while. Please honour your tiredness and rest. If you are doing something and get suddenly tired; please stop for half an hour to an hour's rest. You will then be ready to restart again. It is rather like 'hitting a wall' of tiredness. If you try to push through this 'wall', you can make yourself much more tired.

These are the normal or standard modes of medical practice in the Western world at this time. I am sure that your physician is very knowledgeable about these different methods and he/she and your oncologist will give you answers to all your questions.

One thing I do want to say and say with great emphasis is to follow your physicians and oncologists suggested course of treatment. Once you have received some or all of these treatments you then have a period of time healing and recovery. You will be reassessed and reviewed to see how well you have responded to the treatment(s). Your review sessions may well spread out in frequency from monthly to years. When you are in a period of time where there is no new symptom or further complication you are considered to be in remission. If a re-occurrence of the tumour happens, more surgery, radiotherapy or chemotherapy may be considered. Sometimes, the cancer spreads to other parts of the body. Where the spread occurs is called metastasis. For example, you could have initially experienced breast cancer but some cancer cells spread via your lymph nodes in your armpits to other parts of the body and may lodge and grow in the lung, bone or brain. That is why it is important to get treatment as soon as you think you have a suspicious lump anywhere in your body because the smaller it is the easier it is to treat and the less likely you are to have complications such as metastasis. At some point, you hopefully will be told that the cancer is totally gone and to go and celebrate and enjoy your life. This could be months or even several years after the initial treatment. So during this period of time, you are in a state of uncertainty, not knowing if you are fully healed or not.

Sadly, there will be a small percentage of you that will be told that the cancer has come back, re-occurred, and that there is nothing further that medical science can do for you. At this point, you are usually referred to palliative or end-of-life care. Doctors and nurses who specialise in palliative care are experts in their field. They will be open to discussing all your fears, worries and support you in many ways. This includes medical and nursing care, pain medication to reduce as much pain as possible yet allowing you to function. You may use hospice centres which are specialist care centres where staff are expert in treating people who are dying. You may go in and out of hospice over several months if you need extra support. Some people choose to die in a hospice but many prefer to die at home while receiving expert care from various organisations.

There are many books written about cancer and palliative, end of life and hospice care. Your own doctor or nurse may well have books they recommend or organisations that can be informative and supportive. You may well hear about *The Five Stages of Grief* described by Swiss psychiatrist Elisabeth Kubler-Ross, M.D., whom I heard speak in Sydney Australia. This was first proposed in her book *On Death and Dying*. These stages are listed as Denial, Anger, Bargaining, Depression and Acceptance. The patient and loved ones can go through any or all of these stages. This may be in linear order or moving back and forth with all of them.

Most countries have a main national organisation for cancer that can give you information. Also, there are smaller organisations that provide information, counselling and support groups. Some provide nursing care in the home and hospice care. Most illnesses have an organisation that provides specific information and support for that particular condition.

Complementary (Integrative) Therapies

Everything that I am going to discuss in more detail in this chapter is about healing the whole of you, rather than only focusing on curing the diseased part of you.

You are a human being with a body, head, arms, legs, mind and spirit, not just a blood disorder or tumour in your breast or prostate that needs to be fixed.

Depending on your land of origin, it could be more normal for you to be treated by acupuncturists and herbalists rather than by a Western medical doctor. It is also sometimes called Eastern medicine as an alternate description from Western medicine. Acupuncture, acupressure, herbal remedies and other therapies that we call complementary or alternative medicine (CAM) here in the Western world are often the 'normal' in Eastern cultures.

In the distant past, in the Western world, herbalists were more revered than surgeons who were barbers by profession and surgeons on the side!

Complementary and alternative medicine (CAM) is very interesting and I believe beneficial to the whole healing process and may well enhance your chances of the ultimate cure. However, I believe that the term 'alternative' is an inaccurate label and can be misleading. It infers a concept of either one type of treatment or another, rather than integrating both Western traditional orthodox medicine AND Eastern approaches.

The more appropriate terms are 'CAM', or 'Integrative therapy' or holistic therapy. These are all terms that are 'umbrella' labels for therapies other than orthodox Western medical treatments.

Using both orthodox and non-orthodox approaches simultaneously, is a holistic or whole approach which maximises the chance of surviving and becoming cured/healed.

When we talk about curing, we are talking about fixing someone's disease process and hopefully making them better. When we currently talk about curing patients who have a life-threatening illness, the hope is that the disease will be eliminated and the person will live. The possibly terminal illness will be vanquished and the patient will survive.

In Western medicine, if we can't 'fix' the physical body and cure the patient we feel as if we have failed, or the system has failed or we don't have the right drug or treatment to give. Having done everything medically appropriate, over many months or years, the patient then gets told there is nothing more that can be done. The patient is then deemed terminal and transferred to palliative care and possibly hospice, to prepare to die.

But what if healing does not mean making the physical body well, as Western medicine understands it? What if healing really means taking care of the physical body as best we can and at the same time taking care of the mind, mental state or psyche, and the emotional, spiritual aspects that we all have.

By doing this, we can become more complete, more whole, more satisfied with the way we are living our lives.

Maybe it was unconsciously being unhappy, stressed or not at ease with our life or life choices that was a contributor towards our disease?

Healing the whole of us, body mind and spirit heals the spiritual hole or 'void' that we have, the sense of emptiness, the feeling of, 'Is this what life is all about?' It would be great if this healing could occur prior to our death. So when it is our time to die and leave the body, we can feel that we have made the most of the time we had on Earth.

How can we empower ourselves to meet this challenge? By making informed choices around your care, you will feel more in control. By deciding to embrace everything you want in order to get well or whole.

How is this achieved? I used to live in the Bay Area of San Francisco, which has access to a variety of complementary methods of healing. Other areas of the country and the world are not quite so lucky, so my aim here is to let you know of some of the many therapies that are available to you. I believe that by reading a little about different options will give you some information quickly and easily. If you feel attracted, or drawn, to one or two or three methods you will then be able to further research the topics that interest you the most. I believe that getting information is the source of knowledge. Finding out that something exists and is attainable to you will help empower you in the process of your healing.

Medicine can help you along the way and do the best that it can, but you ultimately are the ruler of your life, and only you can choose how you wish to be treated.

There are so many 'complementary therapies' and more being developed that it would be an impossible task for me to go into each one in detail. My aim is to give you information about the more well-established and traditional ones in a summary fashion. The aim is so that you will become aware of it and can decide if you wish to pursue a method in more detail. The list that I will be giving you is to enable you to find out more about the topics I cover and then to go from there.

Among the many methods of healing therapies are acupuncture, acupressure, herbal medicine, chiropractic, osteopathy, body massage, aromatherapy, touch therapies, meditation, mindfulness, visualisations, breathing techniques, Bowen technique, music and sound therapy, humour therapy, dream therapy and yoga.

I saw in my nursing practice a patient, who I will call Jane, a 35-year-old lady. She had been diagnosed with breast cancer and had undergone a breast removal (called a mastectomy), and had received some, but not all, of her chemotherapy treatment. She decided, for her own reasons and against medical advice to discontinue her chemotherapy treatments and started eating a macrobiotic diet. She was convinced that this was all that she would need to cure her. One day she came to my clinic and she was positively radiant. She was glowing and so excited and she told me that 'God has cured me'. She had attended a church service and had gone to the altar and been 'touched' by God and had felt total love overwhelm her. She was so happy and she was convinced she was well and the cancer was gone.

She certainly looked better than I had ever seen her and I had known her about six months. Sadly, a month or so later, Jane was dead. Some might say 'Well she wasn't cured was she?' And in truth she wasn't. She still had her cancer and unfortunately her cancer eventually lead to her death.

However, was she healed? I believe that her mental and spiritual being was healed. She had had a change of spirit, a change of mental outlook; and through her belief in her macrobiotic diet and God's healing of her, she had contentment and was at peace with her life.

Was she right to turn her back on Western medicine? She was the one who made the choice and we cannot judge what was right for her. However, I wish that she had embraced it all. I wish that she had kept on with her chemotherapy and done whatever else she wished to at the same time.

I believe it is not a matter of 'EITHER – OR' but a 'YES – AND' attitude that we need to encourage.

I want to promote the idea of following Western medical advice and, at the same time that the person is undergoing traditional treatment, they can embrace complementary/alternative therapies that feel 'right' for them – using everything to their advantage!

Healing the whole being, body-mind-spirit, is not necessarily curing. It is a healing of the body-mind-spirit connection in order to promote wellness of the whole of you.

Psychoneuroimmunology (spirit-mind health resulting in improved body immunity response) is a relatively new science. The concept is if one can develop a positive mind and positive attitude through methods such as meditation, visualisations, yoga and diet, reducing some of the stress the person has. Then the body's immune response can be made more effective and improve the body's ability to defend itself against the invading viruses, bacteria or cancer. It can also help to minimise the side effects of the treatment.

Complementary or integrative therapies encompass this area of body-mind-spirit connection by encouraging the person to see themselves as a whole being, and in so doing enhances and promotes the potential for maximum healing.

Touch Therapies

Touch and its importance to man tends to be underrated and not thought about on a conscious level. Touch is a very powerful force that we all need. We laugh and talk of needing a hug a day, 'Have you hugged your dog/cat today?'; car bumper stickers or hand out 'hug cards: good for a free hug' are popular.

Think however of the awful pictures we saw of the babies and toddlers in Eastern Europe who, despite being fed enough, were mentally distressed, failing to thrive, emotionally withdrawn and suffering through lack of touch. Those children were not being touched, held or hugged. Their bodily needs were being met, they were in a place with a roof over their heads, they had beds, they were kept clean and dressed and fed but they were not touched. This lack of touch caused suffering mentally and emotionally and ultimately physically by stunted growth and aberrant behaviour.

There have been studies done about the power of touch and some interesting information has come from it. You will trust someone more if they have touched you appropriately. If a person has someone steal a dollar bill from him at a restaurant, when he is sitting between two strangers, he is more likely to think it is the person who did not touch him that stole from him. Even if that touch is just a tap on the arm to ask to pass the ketchup.

If a doctor comes into your hospital room, sits on your bed, touches your arm and leaves after five minutes, you will think and believe that he spent more time with you and paid you more attention than the doctor who comes in, stands at the end of the bed and talks to you for 10 minutes.

Premature babies thrive better and their heart rates slow down (indicating more relaxation and less stress and anxiety) when their mothers hold them or stroke them in the incubator.

We travel so much and so many families are split and separated by jobs, careers, daily life, that the everyday loving touch within families has slipped away.

Sadly, even teachers in our community are fearful of the nurturing touch they used to give children to comfort them.

People are so afraid of being sued that they tend not to want to touch a person who is in distress, such as a collapsed heart attack victim; although there is a 'Good Samaritan Act' that does protect them.

We put our elderly relatives into homes where they are protected and cared for, but are they touched and loved as they would be if they were in our homes with us? The recent pandemic has shown how lack of touch increases patients' confusion and distress. I know that the thing I really missed the most living alone was hugs!

The gentle art of touching someone's arm or shoulder to give comfort, or to 'kiss or rub and make it better' a child's hurt knee, gives us a clue how we use touch to help each other naturally. Healthy appropriate touch is healing, relaxing, nurturing and makes one feel better.

Touch therapy comes in many forms and is called many different things, but I will include here the more common ones.

Massage

There are light-touch methods with smooth sweeping strokes, commonly called Swedish, Escalon or light-touch massage. There are deep-tissue methods where probing strokes are given to the muscles and down to the bone, called deep-tissue work, or Rolfing or Heller work. There are combinations of the two forms, and some profound work can be done with light sweeping touch such as Swedish or Escalon massage. The aim is to relax the muscles and improve circulation, eliminating toxins. The person may become aware of tension, which they are holding in the body that they had not been aware of. Generally speaking, slim athletic bodies prefer deep-tissue work, whereas light smooth strokes are more comfortable for people with body fat.

I have made it a habit of receiving a massage most months because I firmly believe that it keeps me healthy. For example, I have suffered fewer colds! Yet I am often surprised that my massage therapist finds tense, sore muscles. The technique then is to breathe into those areas that are tense as the massage therapist presses into the muscle. By doing so, the pain, or blocked energy, is released and the muscle relaxes, increasing blood flow into the area, improving normal function.

The overall benefit of most massage therapies is to relieve tension in the muscles, resulting in increased circulation, improving the flow of the lymphatic system. There are specialists who focus on the lymph system (the housecleaner of our body and defence system against invading organisms). They do a lymphatic massage to help drain the lymph into the circulation where it can be released from our bodies, thereby decreasing the toxin levels. By stimulating the lymph system, the immune response can be improved, helping us to fight off bacteria, viruses and maybe slow the growth of malignancies or tumours. Be aware that you might get a headache or feel slightly unwell for 24–48 hours after initial treatments as toxins get released from the body. It also feels great and very relaxing and is rejuvenating. A lovely way to pamper yourself and do your body good!

Aromatherapy

The use of essential oils in massage to help relax or invigorate a person is an ancient art form that is being used actively today. Certain herbs, flowers and scents have different effects on us. They may relax or stimulate you. By smelling these scents or having them massaged into our skin can have a subtle positive effect on us. Aroma therapy is currently very popular in Europe and is becoming better known in America.

Energy Work

This is a group of therapies that focuses on the electromagnetic energy field that we are and that surrounds us. Scientists are finding that we are made up of atoms, neutrons and electrons with positive and negative parts of ourselves. If that sounds too strange to you, think about the fact that our very heart contracts by means of positive and negative chemical charges of sodium and potassium ions. Our heart function shows up as an electrical signal known as an EKG or ECG (electrocardiogram). When we are examined by an MRI machine, the first part of the test is to create a magnetic field around us to balance our body field in one direction so that a diagnosis can then be made.

Energy workers primarily work with this concept of positive and negative points in the body and try to improve this electromagnetic energy flow by removing 'blocks' of energy that could be causing pain.

The belief is that when the flow of life energy (the Chinese call this CHI, East Indians call it PRANA), is blocked, then pain and disease can occur.

In Western countries, we tend to give Chi other names such as Universal Energy, Light Energy.

There are different techniques or methods of working with this energy and some of the common names are Reiki, Jin Shin Jitsu, Polarity, Touch for Health, Therapeutic Touch, Spiritual Healing and Laying on of Hands. The concept is for the practitioner to become a channel or conduit and act as an 'antenna' or facilitator for this universal energy that we have and are surrounded by. The practitioner aims to assist more of the flow to enter the patient and help the patient increase his or her energy level, releasing blockages and achieving more of a balance or wholeness of body-mind-spirit. There is usually an experience of deep relaxation, reduced heart rate, warm body sensations and a de-stressing effect. This energy work is becoming common now and more accepted by people.

In American hospitals, especially on the East Coast, Registered Nurses practice Therapeutic Touch (TT) This therapy was developed by Dolores Krieger, PhD, RN, and is part of the treatment plan for patients in some hospitals.

Clinical research studies show patients experience less nausea, have improved appetites, improved sleep, less pain, more normal blood pressure and are generally more relaxed and less stressed after a TT session. These benefits last for several days after a session. Haemoglobin (the part of blood that carries oxygen from the lung to the tissue or cellular level) has been tested before and after a treatment session. The results show an increase in the level of haemoglobin following a session, by a significant amount. The benefit is that more oxygen can be carried by the blood; the increased oxygen level can get to the cellular level via the blood stream and provide increased oxygenation to the wounded area, thereby increasing the healing potential. Patients with ulcers on their legs (open wounds), which can be painful, often note a decrease in pain and discomfort following a session of energy work.

In Great Britain where energy workers or healers are beginning to be used on a regular basis by doctors in family practices, it has been noted by these doctors that overall healing is accelerated. In England, it is fairly common to have Spiritualist Healers go to NHS (National Health Service) hospitals and visit patients for energy healing, with the doctor's permission.

Kirilian photography is able to show us the energy field around people, animals, plants etc. and this energy is commonly called 'The Aura'. There are some people who can see auras without the aid of Kirilian photography. They can see the energies and colours around people and can tell if their energy is withdrawn, contracted or expanded.

In sick people, the aura is noted to be dim and close to the body. With angry people, the aura is seen to show red sparks. In healthy people, the aura is usually bright and can extend out from the body for a few feet in every direction. When people say to you, 'You look great, you have a glow about you', they are probably reacting unconsciously to your aura energy level. We use the phrase, 'He was in my space', or 'he was right in my face' or 'don't stand so close, it makes me uncomfortable' when we are describing a person who is standing in our auric field, which is an extension of us.

I am reminded of parties we attend and someone is talking to us, and if they are standing too close, we tend to step backwards. Then the person usually steps forward because he really wants to convey his viewpoint to you and so the pair of you 'dance' around the room. You stepping backwards and him stepping forward. Depending on the kind of relationship you have with another, you will allow different levels of closeness to you. Hence, lovers will often entwine themselves around each other, friends will often touch each other.

There is a lovely story I heard of a class of children who were asked to draw and then paint a picture of their family pet. When the teacher went around the class, she saw one girl was painting colours around the outside of the dog's outline. The teacher told her that she should colour inside the dog's outline, not outside. You see, the child was able to see the auric field of her dog, and was painting that!

If you still have a problem believing that you are energy, try this exercise: Rub your two palms together in a fast circular motion for a minute. Now *slowly move* your hands apart a foot or so and then back together again without your palms touching. Do this several times back and forth and you will probably feel a sensation like a cotton wool ball, or taffy building up between your hands.

What you are feeling is the energy of your aura building up between your two hands. When you have energy work or massage, you may feel a variety of energy sensations such as heat, cold, warmth, tingling; these are all interpretations of energy moving through you.

Acupuncture/Acupressure/Reflexology

These treatments are different in application but similar in concept. The Chinese, Oriental, Eastern Medicine practitioners believe that pain and disease are caused by blocks in our energy fields, preventing smooth running of energy/Chi. The aim is to release these blocks by various methods.

Acupuncture: It is the inserting of fine needles (that may or may not be stimulated by motion, vibration or heat) into specific skin points of the body for a short period of time. This is not usually painful and sterile needles are used each time. I would recommend that you choose a fully trained acupuncturist who has completed a four- or five-year training, rather than a medical professional/physical therapist who can legally practice acupuncture after just a few weekend courses.

Ear acupuncture: The ear represents different parts of your body. Needles are placed in these specific areas to help your body. (Similar to Reflexology where the feet represent parts of the body and finger pressure, not needles are used.)

Acupressure: This uses 'trigger points' all over the body by pressing into these areas with fingers, elbows or appliances that are pointed, but not needles The places chosen all over the body for acupuncture and acupressure are based on the idea of Meridian Lines. The concept is that there are many lines of energy that run through our body, connecting different parts of us. These are similar to 'electrical circuits'. They pass from the foot to body to shoulder to scalp to hands and fingers (not necessarily in that order!) The meridian endings are found mostly in the fingers and toes.

Reflexology: It is an ancient art that is currently enjoying a revival. Reflexologists press various points on the foot or hand. When they find a 'knot' or tender spot, they press gently at first and up to the point of your tolerance while asking you to breathe in and out, focusing on the spot they are touching. They keep up the pressure until the tenderness diminishes, disappears or the 'knot' releases. The concept is that where they, or you, feel the knot, there is a block somewhere in the relative 'zone area' represented by the point on your foot. So if the middle of your foot is sore to touch, it could indicate a block or problem with your stomach, liver or kidneys. If the arch of your foot is sore, it could indicate back trouble. I have found that when certain points are pressed on my foot, my stomach or gut can start to growl and gurgle as blocked energy is released. This therapy has been used at a major Scottish Children's' Hospital to help children with severe constipation with very good results. Now whether that is the Reflexology or parents' touch or a combination of both – who knows – but it works!

The belief is that we are energy and if blocked energy can cause pain, discomfort and disease, then by finding and releasing these blocks, we can release pain, improve flow of blood to the area, aid muscle relaxation, reduce built up toxins and by so doing, promote health.

Bowen Technique Therapy

This is a relatively new therapy started in Australia in the 1980s. Highly effective and gentle for all ages for multiple conditions. By moving muscles in a certain way, it can help Back-pain, Sciatica, Neck, Shoulder restrictions, Headaches, Balance Problems to name a few conditions. It is also very calming and claims to work on body, emotions and stress. I had a client who found it very calming during his last few months of life and even his wife noticed an improvement after his treatments.

Creative Visualisations/Guided Imagery

This is a conscious technique where people get themselves into a meditative state and deliberately visualise their disease, be it virus, bacteria or tumour. They picture their immune system of white cells, phagocytes, T-cells or helper cells coming to the problem and defeating or killing the 'bad' organism. How the patient visualises this battle is very unique to each person. It may be by loving and embracing the 'sick' part of them, seeing enveloping phagocytes that immobilise the cells; or it could be with guns and lasers of white cells 'blasting' them out of existence. There is no 'wrong' way. It is purely up to the patient that whatever way feels right for him or her is the 'right' way to do it. This is the basis for psychoneuroimmunology – mind over matter, and it does seem to help because the patient feels they have some control, there is something they can do, while going through traditional medical treatment that others do to them. Also immune systems do seem to improve and can be clinically evaluated by checking white cell and T cell counts before and after sessions.

For people who are reading this and saying to themselves, 'I can't do that, I can't visualise or see things'.

I want to reassure you that you may not think that it is something you can do well, but every one of us dreams, either by day or night, so you *do* have that ability. Don't be afraid to explore this avenue. There are experts who do teach 'Guided

Imagery' to people, so they can help guide you initially until you become more practiced and comfortable with it.

Dream Therapy

This is a little less tangible but the concept is that if you can connect with your 'psyche' or unconscious knowing, then you can connect with the wisdom that you have. If you can get insight from meditating and putting yourself into a dream-like state of awareness, why not access and tap into your dreams and see what your 'unconscious' is trying to tell you. This can be done by yourself or by going to a Dream Group, or someone who specialises in Dream Therapy.

Some psychiatrists and psychologists are asking patients to try and remember their dreams, so that more progress can be made in their treatment. There are books in the market place that claim to be able to interpret your dreams by telling you the significance of 'a bridge' etc. I believe that each one of us has to decide what significance the dream symbols hold for us. A bridge for me might mean crossing water, or might mean fear of falling off, depending on my own life history, and what experiences I have had around bridges. I know it's easier to go buy a book and let it tell you the significance the author thinks a bridge has, but I strongly encourage you not to take the easy way out. Explore on your own, or with the help of a trained professional what the significance of bridges, for example, might play in your life, and then put *that context* into your dream interpretation.

The key to working with your dreams is to start to keep a dream journal. Have a notebook by your bed and if you wake up during the night or in the morning, write down *any* image, memory or feeling that you can recall about the dream you just had. Starting to write, even just a feeling, acts as a trigger for your subconscious to feed you more information about the dream and you will find that you are able to remember more and in greater detail than before you started writing. As you do this over time, you will find patterns emerging, themes that may well have meaning for you. Some people, before they go to sleep, write down the day's events and how they are feeling on the left page of the notebook, and the dreams they had that night on the right page with a summary of the dreams interpretation below that.

Yoga/Breath Work

Yoga practices' are varied; some focus on body posture and stretches. Some are more meditation focused, sitting in certain positions and working with the breathe to help relax, release emotions and increase the sense of overall wellness. The main theme is to improve your state of well-being, mentally, emotionally and physically.

Sound Therapy

Sound can be used as an aid to help release emotions, move energy and enhance or deepen relaxation, depending on the type of music, or sound. The deeper, rhythmic sound of beating drums gives a different energy in comparison with sounds of the ocean, or mood music. The use of music, someone making sounds around you or you making sounds can be a very powerful experience. Some massage therapists are using sounds or 'sounding' as part of their practice, and most of them use music as a tool for assisting relaxation.

Humour Therapy

Over the last few years, this therapy has become a well-established concept. The phrase 'Laughter is the best medicine' has been proven to be true. Laughter causes the stomach and abdominal organs to be massaged by the rib cage, abdominal muscles to expand and contract aiding lymph movement. Endorphins are released which make you feel better as they are the natural 'feel good' hormones that we can produce in our bodies. If you laugh till the tears roll down your face, it can be a tremendous release of tension. A good old belly laugh is good for you! Nowadays, there are classes in laughter, they 'ha ha' and 'ho ho ho' themselves into feelings of well-being.

Colour Therapy

The use of colour can affect your mood and how you feel. Some colour therapists are using all colours of the spectrum to assist in healing. They use special colour filters in their offices to promote different emotions, feelings and energies. They have people use certain colours both in their houses, and with the clothes they wear. You can purchase light bulbs that have coloured hues that help create a feeling of warmth or coolness to a room. After having a lung condition, I thought I would assist the healing by 'thinking a green colour' into my lungs, as green is one colour of healing. Now this may sound strange, but as I started to think green, I 'heard' in my head 'blue please'. It seemed that my lungs wanted blue to be visualised, so I listened to my inner voice and went with blue!

Herbal Remedies

There is a whole science around the use of herbs to help various physical, mental and emotional conditions. Acupuncturists often use them to supplement their therapy. Naturopathic and Homeopathic Practitioners use essences of flowers and herbs in diluted amounts to help improve the condition of the patient. The base remedy that they use comes from pure flower, plant or herb extract or essences. One of the most well-known ones is Bach Flower Remedies, made by Nelson Pharmacy in London, UK, but there are others available. 'Rescue Remedy' is a Bach Flower Remedy that can help emotional shock. It is found in many chemists and pharmacies in the United Kingdom. I have found that it can help after an accident or shock event by calming me.

Meditation

This was initially a specialty of the Hindu and Buddhist religions that has now spread worldwide, and there are many different forms and names given for the various techniques practiced by people. I use the word 'practice' deliberately because it requires regular repetition, in order to fully feel the benefits. The aim for all the various methods though is the same, and ultimately you can explore some of the different ways and decide what feels right for you. The aim is to 'turn inward' to close your eyes and explore the inner part of you; finding out what makes you 'tick'.

There is a saying that you can go see many masters, teachers or gurus, but in the end the journey starts and ends with you. You have the wisdom that you need, you just need to 'go inside' and seek it.

The practice is to find a quiet space in your home or to create a special place that can be considered a place where you go to meditate. Similar to you going to bed to sleep, so you go to your special chair, room, area of a room where you will practice the art of meditation.

The common theme of all the practices is to get into a position of being receptive, quiet and focusing on your inner self, or inside yourself. The Bible talks of 'being still and listening to that inner small voice inside of yourself'. 'Be still and know that I am God'.

The aim is to mentally become quiet, slow down, stop the mental running or self-talk that our mind tends to do and to be open for answers to questions we may have that our unconscious may be able to give us. We are looking for 'In-sight' and we have to go inside ourselves to get it.

There is a saying 'Prayer is when you talk to God and Meditation is when God talks to you' People often say 'I don't know how to meditate' because they have heard there is only one way to do it or that you need to have a 'mantra' (a word or sound given to you by your spiritual teacher or guru).

It does not need to be that complicated, but you may be more comfortable getting guidance or having structure around your practice. You may want to go and join others who meet and meditate together.

The common factors are:

1. Being in a quiet room, alone, where you will not be disturbed. Turn off the TV, radio and telephone.
2. Sit with a straight back, eyes closed and your hands resting in your lap, elbows slightly bent. Comfort is important, so adapt this position as you need to. Use a chair, bed, lie flat if you prefer with limbs uncrossed and palms upwards or comfortably resting on your lap.
3. Try to quiet your mind – this is the hardest part. You can choose to focus on your breath and feel it passing into your nose and into your lungs and then easily passing back out again past the tip of your nose. As you find yourself traveling off from thinking about your breathing to thoughts of your day, concerns, jobs to do, let that go and gently bring your focus back to your breathing.
4. Do not get caught up in thoughts of 'I can't do this', 'Am I doing it right?' Just let yourself drift on the focus of breathing out and in. I say focus on breathing out for that is a passive action, it just happens and then by breathing out, you have to breathe in.

5. The aim is to quiet the daily mind chatter that we all have from the moment we wake up until we go to sleep. The hope is that during the phase of 'mind quiet' that we are trying to achieve, we may get some peace, a sense of mental expansion, a feeling of being larger than our physical body. In that state, we can connect with the Universe or God. This phase of expansion and of feeling connected with something greater than ourselves can be called a sense of enlightenment, a sense of being whole, at one, united body-mind-spirit. Some call it a state of being aware or 'conscious'. Some belief systems label it as Samadhi, a state of God-union. They believe only 'holy' men or their 'disciples' or followers of their discipline or way of practice can achieve this state of expanded awareness. I believe any of us, with regular practice, can achieve this very pleasant expanded state of awareness.
6. While in this level of expanded awareness, we can get inspiration, some answers to our questions that maybe our linear way of thinking was not able to achieve. We get a sense of well-being, or wholeness, we may see visions, see our higher, knowing self, get a message from the inner wisdom that we have.
7. When we feel that we have sat long enough, or received all we need to know for the time being, we can gently come back to a regular level of conscious awareness, becoming aware of our body's boundaries, the feel of our feet on the ground, the presence of the room around us. We can take a few minutes to 'come to', so that we don't feel light-headed, and can go on with the rest of the day.

The 'gift' we bring back with us from the meditation session is the information, ideas, feelings and peace that we experienced in those moments and they can enrich our everyday conscious awareness. The experience can give us reassurances, wisdom, insight, a sense of peace and calm that otherwise we might not have.

The physical benefits of meditation have been scientifically documented and include slowing of the breath, slowing of the heart rate, decreased pain awareness, or increased tolerance of pain. Blood pressure is lowered, sleep is deeper and less fragmented and the person is less stressed. I know personally that when I take the time out to meditate, I feel so much better and my day appears to go more smoothly. I seem to be able to relate to others on a different level, have less fear or worry less about 'stuff' and am more emotionally and mentally calm and 'centred' or 'grounded'.

Yet despite all the benefits that I know it brings, one of the hardest things for me to do is to find the time in my day to do it. It only needs a minimum of 10–15 minutes as you start practicing, but it is so alien for us to remove ourselves from the hustle and bustle of our crammed busy days, and take a few minutes for ourselves. I find it, like exercise, one of the first things I let go of when I'm stressed or busy, yet it is probably the more important thing I can do to help de-stress myself. You will discover, as you do more meditation that time becomes altered. You may think that only 15 minutes has gone by, but actually 30 minutes have flown by! Some people after a length of time practicing meditation may do as much as 1–2 hours daily or several days a week. I do not recommend alarm clocks. I find that I can state out loud that I want the meditation to stop at 2 pm, for example, and I open my eyes at 2 pm!

I recently heard of the image of meditating as allowing time for cloudy, sandy water to settle to the bottom of a bowl so that clear water could rise to the surface.

Prayer and inspiration can then occur, with the clarity of an open mind.

There is also mindfulness meditation that encourages being aware or 'conscious' as we go through our day.

The Power of Prayer

Different faiths will pray in different ways. They will use prayer to appeal to various saints such as St Peregrine who had cancer himself and healed many people. Or, St Rafael, the angel of love and healing mentioned in the *Book of Tobit* in the Apocrypha. They may go to shrines such as Lourdes for healing. People may light candles, chant, ring bells and turn prayer wheels. The one thing in common is turning to a Higher Power, God, Allah or Source outside of yourself, to ask for help with your healing.

The energy of prayer and intercession sends a wave of positive energy somewhere into the ethers.

There have been some well-documented studies into the positive effect of prayer.

In San Francisco, California, in a Coronary Care Unit, where patients had just had a heart attack were admitted, they were alternately allocated to Group A or Group B. Group A was prayed for several times a day by volunteers who did not know the names of the people they were praying for. The patients in Group A also did not know they were being prayed for. At the end of six months, Group A statistically had better overall results: less pain, less drug interventions, less complications, quicker and better recovery compared with Group B. So if this appeals to you – ask friends, church, pastors to pray for you. Create a prayer circle or support circle for yourself and others that need it or feel that it might benefit them.

Spend 5–10 minutes a day in formal prayer or informally speak to God and listen for guidance, through thoughts that come to you. This will hopefully increase your inner peace. A spiritually positive approach aids healing as we are spirit encased in a human body.

There are many forms of prayer, formal and informal, affirmations, positive messages. The Lord's Prayer, Prayers to Catholic Saints. Islamic, Jewish, Hindu, Buddhist religions all have their special prayers and rituals. One prayer or affirmation that I like is the Serenity Prayer:

> Grant me the *Serenity* to accept the things I cannot change,
> *Courage* to change the things I can,
> And the *Wisdom* to know the difference.

Other sayings/affirmations also help. I list a few from the 12-Step programs:

> Serenity is not freedom from the storm but Peace amid the Storm
> Take it one day at a time
> Let Go and Let God (help)
> God never gives you more than you can handle

'Footprints in the Sand' is an inspirational reading: I was reviewing my life and saw two pairs of footprints in the sand, and then I saw that during the hard parts of my life, you abandoned me God; there was only one set of footprints in the sand. God replies, 'My child, where there were only one set of footprints, I was carrying you!'

I was asking God 'Why don't you help me'

God replies 'My Child, I tried to help, but you never would let go!'

Gratitude Journal

Have an 'attitude of gratitude', despite what is going on in your life. Why?

By making note of what good things have happened to you today, like someone smiling at you, giving you a compliment, or try being thankful for what you have, a roof over your head, food on the table, family and friends. By writing down three things you are grateful for each night in a journal, it 'cements' it into your subconscious. This energy focus of positivity, helps lift negative thoughts or sense of limitation. It shifts the focus and lessens the impact of 'I have cancer... will I survive?' as you fall asleep, thus helping to reduce some of the stress and worry.

Taking Care of Yourself

You are a precious child of God. You are going through a horrid time and you did nothing to deserve this. You may well be asking 'Why me?' Then you may get to a place where you ask 'Why not me?'

How you take care of yourself is important. Take time to nourish yourself during this difficult time. Get extra rest, have good nutrition, give yourself treats, pamper yourself. By taking care of yourself, you will have more strength to fight the disease process and hopefully get a full recovery, body, mind and spirit.

Sacred Space

This is a concept that was taught to me recently. When you have to go into the hospital as an inpatient and stay overnight, or especially if you are there for a few days or weeks, it is important to create **your** space as much as possible. Take with you articles that remind you of your normal life and are important to you. Hospitals can be very impersonal and bringing with you reminders of home can help you deal with the different situation. This can be personal 'home' articles, or a series of photos, things that have special meaning to you. You can hang them up on the walls or on the ceiling and they will help remind you that you are part of a different community, that your real life is not the hospital room but elsewhere. For those of you facing a lengthy stay, I urge you to try to get a room with a view, preferably looking out at nature, but at least be in a room that has a window looking out so that you can see day time and night time. It has been noted that people who stay in hospital for more than a few days get depressed and disoriented if they can't see outside. If you like the American Indian concept of East representing or meaning fresh starts, birth, new beginnings; South meaning warmth and growth; West being transition, loss and letting go; and North being trials, cold, hardships, you could put pictures that represent these things for you up on the appropriate walls of your room, like a collage. By using something such as 'blue tack', you will not upset the hospital by ruining the paint on the walls. You can include Heaven and Earth by hanging something significant (like an angel, or stars) to your overhead bed rail or light. Have flowers or plants in the room, artificial ones if real ones are not permitted. Have some comedy videos/DVDs for your 'humour therapy'! Whatever works for you, to make your hospital room feel as much like a safe, home-like environment, do it! It will make you feel better and hopefully speed up the rate of your recovery.

Addictions

Trying to get healthy includes looking at substance abuse, such as overuse of alcohol, food, smoking and drugs. I am not talking about pain medications that are needed and medically prescribed. By addressing negative coping skills, your quality of life can be improved.

Twelve-Step Programmes can be very helpful, some friends, counselling, support systems. Try to search out ways of coping in life changing ways.

All the things that I have mentioned in this chapter are suggestions for ways to help you through difficult times. As some wise people have said 'Take what you like and leave the rest'. I would encourage you to read more about the areas that interest you and then go and try out some of the therapies. What do you have to lose? Think how much you might gain!

Please do not use these complementary integrative therapies as a substitute for Western Medical treatment; but as an additional help.

Use everything to your advantage, so you can maximize your healing potential

Research and ask questions. Never 'ASSUME' – that makes an ASS out of You and ME

When you can't control becoming ill, control the way you respond.

Chapter 5

'Please Put Yourself in My Shoes, Doctor'

Currently in the healthcare industry, there is a habit of giving negative news and information in a minimised way. The inference is that if you just get the facts out and then talk positively about what wonderful things medicine can do, then the patient will go away feeling reassured and you, the doctor, will also feel better because you gave the patient negative news in a positive way.

Medicine hates to admit that maybe there is no cure, or that they cannot help in some way. In order to best cope with this, the theme seems to be to minimise the telling of the negative test result, maximise the cure, minimise the possibility of death and focus on the 'fix'.

If there is no cure, then send the patient off to palliative care where experts can discuss death and dying because they are familiar and comfortable with the topic, as it is their specialty.

When we as a society are not comfortable with death, we fail to train our doctors and nurses in being comfortable with it and they have to manage the best they can. As with anything, if you are not comfortable with your own life, death and mortality, how can you be comfortable with others?

So 'least said' is the form of managing to give someone difficult uncomfortable news.

Much easier to say 'Don't worry, you'll be alright, we'll take care of you', than to have to say 'I'm sorry but you have a condition that might or will kill you in the near future'.

How often as healthcare providers do we say to people, 'Don't worry, the success rate is high, so let us not talk about death and dying because I'm sure you won't have to face that, so let us talk positively'. These patients then go home, back to their life, and their number one focus will probably be 'Am I going to die?' They may well not speak this fear out loud, and their family and friends probably will go along with the idea of being positive. The patient is wondering about death and dying but doesn't bring it up with their family or friends, because it may be too difficult to face. They don't want to appear pessimistic and they don't want to worry their loved ones. However, in their mind, the concern and worry runs along like an undercurrent. 'Will I make it? Joe down the street had "IT" and he died, what will stop me from dying, what's so different?' In this day and age, there are still people who can't bring themselves to talk about 'IT'. As if to talk about death, dying or the big 'C' word, it could be catching or come sooner.

So we need to focus on the number one issue of 'Am I going to die?' right up front, immediately or very soon after diagnosis. Bring that fear right out into the open, encourage patients and friends to talk about their concerns, and help them with their learning about the possibilities. If faced in the light of knowledge, the 'Death Dragon (DD)' (see Chapter 2) will be seen to be a lot smaller that if it is allowed to be in the darkness of silence.

By tackling this issue as soon as possible, the patient's level of fear can be reduced and the patient can focus more energy on positive thoughts that can go towards healing and hopefully recovery.

People tend not to talk about death until the patient is pronounced terminal. Then the family members may start talking about death. Hospice might get involved and bring up death and dying as a topic. However, it can be months or years from the initial diagnosis to terminal-stage prognosis and why should patients have to suffer unnecessarily in silence (self-imposed or not) with the fear of possibly dying from the illness that they have. Usually people don't have that fear addressed until months and years have gone by. Yet the fear of the 'DD' has been lurking in the shadows or forefront of their mind since their diagnosis.

Breaking the stress cycle early on, just after initial diagnosis, by talking about the fear of dying, death and the possibilities; allowing the patient, partner, friend to talk about their concerns **if they want to**, I believe can reduce stress, worries and feelings of isolation. This promotes healing and eases the path right from the start of treatment instead of months or years later.

I have seen and heard some negative stories of how well-meaning doctors have informed their patients of cancer or some life-threatening illness as if it is almost an insignificant thing that he or she will fix. Rather like 'Oh, your car needs to have an oil change; don't worry we'll do it next week and it will be fine'.

One story I heard about was a gynaecologist who entered a three-bed ward of the hospital and went to the middle bed. There was his patient, a 32-year-old mother of two, who had come in for tests on her uterus for possible cancer. Without pulling the screen round her bed, getting a chair to sit beside her or hold her hand, without taking her into another room to give her privacy, he stood at the end of the bed and said, 'Mrs Smith, your test has come back positive. I will take you to the Operating Room tomorrow for a hysterectomy and I'm sure you will be fine after that. Not to worry, you are in good hands'. With that said, he left the ward.

Mrs Smith meanwhile has been given, to her, earth shattering news. She was given no privacy, no time to ask questions, no time to think, before he left the room. Now I'm sure people might say, 'Well he is probably busy, must not bother the doctor, don't make a fuss, just got to get on with it. After all, he knows best and he's probably done lots of these kinds of surgeries'.

Mrs Smith is sitting in the bed probably stunned and numb. All her worst fears of cancer, surgery, losing her uterus, not being able to have more children, are now realised. Is she going to survive the surgery? Will there be a scar? What if the cancer has spread? Will she die of secondaries in two- or three-year time? Will she see her children grow up? All these thoughts are crowding her brain. Yet she is in the middle of a ward, stuck between two strangers, so she must not 'lose it', she must appear calm.

She gets out of bed, hurries to the bathroom where she closes the door and at last can do whatever she needs to do, cry, sit in stunned shock, whatever. As she does that, the two other patients may talk to each other about what just happened. Her confidentiality is totally blown, but much more than that is the appalling way in which she was treated by her surgeon.

Personally, if that had been me as the patient, I would not have let him near me again. I would have got a second opinion and have gone on from there.

I am sure that some of you are saying to yourselves, 'Oh that could never happen', but believe me it did; although I grant you that it is somewhat rare, thank goodness.

In fairness to the doctor, he probably thought his actions were reasonable. Get the information out as quickly and briefly as possible, minimise the impact by going immediately to the fact that surgery was the answer to the problem and reassure the patient that you are a good surgeon.

Another tale I have is of a woman who is newly diagnosed with breast cancer. For some reason, the surgeon who has done the breast biopsy and has received the results is not going to do the surgery. He passes the patient's case file to another surgeon who calls the patient up on the phone, at home on a Friday evening, and says, 'I am Dr Brown. Dr Jones has asked me to take your case on. I will be doing your mastectomy next Wednesday. Then you will have chemotherapy and then you will be fine. Don't worry, you can even get an artificial reconstructed breast if you want to afterwards and so there is nothing to worry about'.

As the patient told me, the doctor had not checked with her if it was alright to give her the news over the phone and his whole attitude had been very casual. She had not been given the diagnosis prior to the doctor's phone call; he had not checked if talking to her at that time was convenient to her. As she said, she could have had guests over for dinner and she would have had to get off the phone and cope through a dinner party after having been given that news.

Needless to say, she opted to see another surgeon, but she told me later that he had not been much better. He had come into the exam room, told her he would do the surgery, followed by chemotherapy and then discussed breast reconstruction possibilities with her.

As she said, he never once shook my hand or touched me. He made me feel that I was just another case in his busy day. I am facing a life-threatening diagnosis of breast cancer, I am about to lose a breast, which for many women is an identifying part of their femininity, and I felt like he'd given me the facts. I was a straightforward case and what was I worrying about? I felt that I should not make a fuss.

We have to stop and realise what we are telling these patients. It may just be another mastectomy to us, but to that one woman, it is the first time she has ever lost a breast.

It is one of her worst fears coming true, and she may survive the surgery, but will she survive the illness? Will her husband or partner still love her?

There is the pressure of time that we all have and those of us in the healthcare industry are just as rushed as other professionals and workers. Avoidance of the possibility of dying and death is human. We can use the excuse of business, think positive, don't dwell on the morbid, but we should realise that people need more from us than that.

Have you ever received an incorrect tax bill on a Friday night and you know that there is nothing you can do about it until Monday? Two days is a long, long time when you can't ask questions or get things straightened out. So imagine if you are given a diagnosis of a life-threatening illness on a Friday afternoon? Or imagine you are in the middle of a lunch party when the phone rings and you are given negative information and you have to continue through the luncheon acting as if everything is just fine, when in reality your whole world has just changed.

I think it is vital that when a person is given a life-threatening diagnosis, that it is done face to face, with time given for handholding, tissue offering and a hug given if appropriate. You may say this already happens, but it does not. I have recently had two male friends complain that they have felt they were being talked down to at the time of diagnosis. One young doctor spoke *at* the patient, not *to* the patient. 'I felt like I was being treated as a three years old instead of the 60-year-old intelligent man that I am'. The other friend said that he felt that his doctor, who was a lady, was being patronising and condescending with him. She patted his hand and said, 'There there, not to worry dear. You'll be fine and we will take good care of you'. He is 68 and the doctor in her early 30s. He was furious at her attitude. Don't assume one way is the right way. Show them the dignity that you would like to receive. Treat them as an equal and learn from them.

Yes, it is uncomfortable, yes, you want to impart the information as soon as possible and remove yourself from this uncomfortable position, but this a human being's life you are talking about. It is a bad-enough situation that the patient has to go through, so let us make it a good experience.

One patient's impression when she was told of her breast cancer was, 'I felt like a number'. The doctor walked into the room, recited diagnosis and treatment. Then, in the same breath, that I 'could get a breast reconstruction so I'd be alright'.

It was so matter of fact. I felt I was a case to be dealt with and treated: 'Take a number and stand in line'. I have never had cancer before, the very word filled me with dread and I wanted him to stop and take a breath and look at me. I wanted him to stop reciting facts that in that instant I could not absorb. I wanted to say to him, 'Would you mind showing me you care? You see, this might be your hundredth cancer case, but it is my first time, so please be gentle with me'.

By giving the diagnosis and then having the patient come back in the next few days to talk about treatment gives the patient time to get over the numbing initial shock. I would encourage you to give a diagnosis and hold a hand on one visit. Then on the next visit, discuss treatment options, and ask for questions and openly ask about their fears. 'How are you dealing with this?'

You might say, 'You have cancer and I'm sure you are probably a little concerned about the possibility of dying, so let's talk about that', or 'Maybe the possibility of death is on your mind. Would you care to talk about it?' Or 'Let's get the fears and concerns you may have about death and dying out into the open where we can discuss it'.

'Are you alright? How are **you** (the person) doing?' Then say, 'Let's talk about your illness'. These are two separate issues.

Let's start making it the normal routine to talk about fears of dying shortly after diagnosis. Why? Because you are assisting in bringing a non-verbal, worrying, negative energy to the surface, into the open. Getting it out into the open can help address the patient's fears so that he or she can get to release some of that fear, reduce some of their stress and improve their healing potential.

By getting this information, the patient can then choose what they believe (take what you like and leave the rest). Having permission to discuss it, think about it and have choices, empowers them and increases a sense of control.

By early discussion of the probability of fear in the patient, right after diagnosis, allows it to come out into the open. We 'get it off our chest' and by doing so, the power it has over us is diminished. So the patient can reduce their anxiety and focus more on the healing of their body, mind and spirit early on in the disease process and not wait until the 'terminal' stage.

Let's change these well-known closed statements:

1. You have cancer, but do not worry, you will be fine.
2. Don't talk about death, you are being morbid.
3. Let's not talk about death until we absolutely have to.
4. Why are you worrying, the success rate is 90%.

Change these statements to be more open-ended ones:

1. You have cancer and I'm sure you are probably concerned a little about the possibility of dying, so let us talk about those fears if you would like to.
2. Obviously, the possibility of death is on your mind, would you like to talk about it?
3. Let us get the fears and concerns you may have about death and dying out into the open where we can talk about them. This may help you focus more on healing and getting well.

4. The reason for talking about your fears as soon as you are ready to do so is to let you express them; then you will be able to get on with living and give yourself the best chance at life. We have found that by talking about the possibility of death and dying, patients have less stress around that issue and can then focus more on getting well. Just let me know when you are ready to do that.
5. Would you like to talk about anything that we have not covered?
6. Even though the success rate is 90% and I am positive that you will do well, it is only human to worry about that other 10%. So we could, if you like, take a look at your fears of being in the 10% group so that you are then able to focus more on recovery.

Scary isn't it, but we are giving the patient permission to talk about their fears.

Please note that he or she doesn't have to talk; everyone has the choice and some will never be ready to talk about death, even on their deathbed.

Let us start giving the majority of people the green light and not the red light to talk about these fears that they have, so we can reduce fears and stress and promote more healing.

It is scary enough to have the fears and to face the possibility of death and dying without getting verbal and non-verbal messages not to discuss those fears.

Be present, be open and listen, and trust you will know the things to say. If you don't know the answer, you can always say, 'It's tough and I'm sorry you are having to face this, but I think I'd recommend this course of action…'.

This changes a Grade B into an A+ session with the patient, because you have given them hope, physically, mentally and emotionally. You have addressed all three aspects of their well-being.

Help them to feel that you care, that you are sorry that they have to deal with this. You could say, 'It isn't nice or fun and life can be hard but maybe something good will come of this episode in your life. This may be a time you can learn more about yourself. There are various options and views and additional therapies beyond traditional Western medicine that you could utilise in addition, if you chose to'.

What freedom for the patient if he or she feels they can turn to you and say, 'What if I don't make the grade, what if I end up kicking the bucket, do you have any guidance for me? I expect you have had others go along this same path, but it is the first time for me and I'd like some advice'.

At that point, if you are not comfortable with talking about the various issues, or time is an issue because let's face it – it is a big issue, maybe let them know about this book. Guide them to any local resources that are in the area such as support groups, a counsellor who specialises in this area, or complementary therapies healing centres. Give them pointers, a guide, a tool to help them in their search for the answers to their questions. Be their support.

You are giving them the opportunity to release their fears, diminish stress, promote healing and immune system strengthening, and hopefully reduce disease.

By avoidance, you deprive them of your expertise. You have seen much more death than your patient.

Take the patient to somewhere quiet and private and give them time. Don't tell them their diagnosis in the middle of a corridor or in a three-bed ward where others are listening and you can make a quick getaway.

Stop minimising what to them is a potential death sentence. Give them the facts by all means, but take time to address the whole being, the human being, the body, mind, spirit personality sitting in front of you.

Stop and think to yourself, 'How would I like to be told? How would I like to be treated? How would I feel?' Be honest with yourself and with your patient. Hold a hand, sit with them, offer a tissue – be human! Say to them, 'Life can be unfair at times' or 'This isn't fun, is it?'.

Talk about their concerns so that the patient can let go of some of his fears and get on with life and living.

Let your patient be the one to decide not to worry or not to talk, but you as the caregiver should give them every opportunity, every bit of help you can to empower them. To assist and help them along their path of treatment and wellness. Bring up the discussion of fears around death; give them information, your opinion to that patient.

Patients always have the ultimate choice; they are the ones with the disease, the ones facing possible death. In the face of adversity, we can be strong if we know what we are up against.

Do the best job you can for your patient and for yourself by helping to light up the path of discovery that the patient will be traveling along during his treatment. By being present in the moment when that patient really needs you, by reaching out to touch, listen, comfort and support isn't that what it's all about? What if people cry or you cry and show your vulnerability? You are human too and it is fine.

The biggest thing people want to do is to be able to help, to feel useful, to feel needed; which is probably why you chose to be in the health professions.

The patient then has his fears addressed early on, directly after the diagnosis is given, if the patient so chooses. They are not hushed up and told to not worry. They are given the space to explore the possibilities and have their fears reduced. How much easier it would be then, if the patient does find out that treatment has not been successful, that they are in fact terminal and facing death in the near future; because so many of the issues have already been addressed.

If, on the other hand, the patient is cured or goes into remission, they have already taken a long hard look at their lives and may have decided that they are not living the way they wish to and can make life changes if they so choose. For by looking at life and death and the possibilities of dying, it makes us look at how we are living now. As one patient of mine said, 'Getting a diagnosis of breast cancer was ultimately the best thing that happened to me. It made me stop and look at what I was doing with my life. Which in turn made me start to love myself more and take care of myself. I realized that I had a limited time of life, cure or no cure, cancer or no cancer, and I decided to make the most of my life and live every moment. After all, this life is not a dress rehearsal; it is happening right now'.

I believe that how we are told and how we are handled at the time of diagnosis can make a major difference to our outlook on the disease and our mortality and our chances of recovery.

The fact is that we in Western medicine have got so far away from the whole person concept and so wrapped up in the scientific fixing or curing of the body, we have forgotten to address the rest of the patient. We focus on symptoms, clinical data and then how to correct the physical findings, ignoring unintentionally the rest of the patient.

We have fragmented the patient. The mind goes to the psychiatrist, the spirit to the priest or minister and the body to the medical doctor. Our focus on the 'fix' of the patient's body and our sense of failure when we don't succeed is a sad indication of how focused we have become about the body and have forgotten about the power of the mind and spirit. To encourage our patients to take care of all of themselves while undergoing Western medical treatment can only be a benefit to them. They look to us for guidance and help when they are sick and it is our responsibility to treat them as a whole human being, not just a medical condition that needs to be fixed!

It is alright to cry, to be vulnerable. It does not mean that you are weak or unprofessional. You are a human being observing the frailty of life and you care. God can speak through us; we may not think we know what to say, or say it right. If we trust that what we are going to say is for the patients higher good and benefit, and if we speak with love and compassion in our hearts, then what we say will be perfect in the moment, for that patient in that moment.

Recently, I burst into tears giving a bereavement card to a patient's wife. I walked into where she worked and handed her the card. I started to say how sorry I was and my tears started. I was so embarrassed because there was nothing I could do to stop them; he had been such a special person. Was she embarrassed or cross? No! She touched her heart with her hand and said, 'This means so much to me. I'm very touched by this', and there were tears in her eyes. We separated a few minutes later, both enriched by the experience; we'd each been touched by the other. That is a soul-to-soul connection. Tears touch us all, they dissipate anger, they let someone know you care or are hurting. So give them the gift of your tears when it feels safe to do so.

That is what life is about, saying hallo to a fellow spirit travelling this learning journey called human life. It may not be the thing to say to another patient; you may need different words or timing for others. We are each and every one of us different, unique and special.

Think Love and then speak. Intimacy – in to me see. See where I am at emotionally. Be there for me and listen….

When healing of the whole person takes place, we see increased calmness and inner peace. Decreased stress, improved sleep, better appetite, lowered pain thresholds and an improved strengthened immune system.

By not saying anything or avoiding the issue, we tend to promote the person's feelings of being abandoned, isolated by family, friends and the medical profession. We need to learn to communicate our care, to listen to the needs of the person and touch their being.

Doctors and nurses sometimes feel they have failed because the patient was not cured. There can be issues of anger, frustration, guilt and inadequacy. Thoughts of 'if only...' The tendency when this occurs is to withdraw oneself from the source of discomfort – namely, the patient.

Instead, acknowledge that death is a normal part of living. Be open to acceptance of death, realising that it is the body that dies. The essence continues on its journey of life.

By encouraging our patients to take care of the whole of themselves whilst undergoing Western medical treatment can only be a benefit to them. They look to us for guidance and help when they are sick and it is our responsibility to treat them as a whole human being.

There is a wonderful movie called 'The Doctor' with actor William Hurt, made in 1991, which I recommend to all doctors and nurses to see. It is based on an expert surgeon who is a little like the aforementioned doctor, and how he suddenly is facing surgery and a life-threatening disease himself and how the tables are turned on him. He decides to choose a caring doctor to take care of him rather than an unapproachable one. It is a very humanising thing to be a patient and I think all medical personnel should have to be a patient before they can practice.

I think that timing of imparting news like that, of cancer and malignancies, should be done when there is time made for it. At the end of the day when no other cases are waiting to be seen, when you can give time for questions, allowing time for fears and tears to be expressed. Some doctors make it a practice to call a patient with the result of breast cancer malignancy and then have the patient come in to the clinic a few days later to discuss treatment after the initial numb shock reaction has worn off. I do agree that there is an immediate numbness and inability to question at the time of being given the result. My thoughts are that to tell a patient over the phone is practical but not very personable.

In the work I did, we made it a practice to be in the room while the doctor gave the patient the result, held the person's hand, or rubbed their back or whatever seemed appropriate in the moment, giving verbal and non-verbal support. The patient was given time to think, ask questions, not rushed. They were encouraged to call us or to come again within a week to discuss issues, have their questions answered and the next phase of care discussed. Also to have time to discuss the possibility of death and the statistics of success rates if treatment was given. The treatment, based on the pathology or type of cancer was discussed at the second visit. At the second visit, the patient has had time to think and gather up questions and thoughts they may have.

At the hospital where I worked, there was a psychiatry department and there were groups that met with the focus on those who had been bereaved. But, and this is a big but, there was nothing for those people who were facing the possibility of death and dying. This is considered normal in most places, but I think that it is wrong!

Death is such a stranger to the majority of us that we have built up this barrier around the whole subject. There are many people who have not seen death, and healthcare providers are in a privileged position of being somewhat familiar with the appearance of death. We can help others by reassuring them that it is not a terrifying event. That it can be a peaceful release, and sometimes a quiet slipping away. I believe that if the patient is willing and if we ask them if they would like to talk about their fears, that this kind of information would be very calming and reassuring.

Once the person has all this information, and can assimilate it, then they can do research if they choose and enlarge and enrich their knowledge base. Then if they find out that they are fully recovered or diagnosed as terminal they will be more informed about death, and the life beyond. Maybe during this search, the person finds wholeness and satisfaction with life and is able to come in touch with their 'reason for being'. What a gift!

For the person diagnosed as terminal, how much more peacefully may they be able to accept the result and ready themselves for death if they have done the research and have the knowledge already.

People who have had a near-death experience (NDE) have universally said that they are no longer afraid to die because they have experienced what it is like, and they realise that death is not to be feared. They have said that by no longer fearing death they were able to enrich and deepen their life experience because they no longer had the fear running them at a subconscious level. The person who has seen what death can be like finds themselves freer to enjoy richer, more fulfilled lives because they have overcome one of mans' deepest fears.

The popularity of the books written about NDE's and the talk circuits, shows that people are hungry to learn more about the 'what if's' of death.

How much hungrier must the person be who has just been given a possible death sentence!

By giving the patient room to express their fears, we put the patient back in control. They are then free to talk about their concerns over death and dying, their fear of pain, change of life expectancy and possible loss of life. They are freer to talk about their anger, to grieve at the unfairness of life, and the situation they have to face and deal with. I have had patients tell me that they never felt *so* alone as they did after their diagnosis, because people would not talk with them normally.

We know that fear increases stress, compromising the healthy balance of the body, contributing to more disease. Fears about survival and death and dying increase stress, not an ideal condition for relaxation and feelings of well-being, which reduce stress, promoting the chances of recovery and healing during and after surgery, chemotherapy and/or radiation.

By reducing the degree of fear, energy that has been used for worrying is now available for the healing process. The amount of energy they expend on fears, resulting in stress, sleepless nights, tiredness, depression, loss of appetite, probably further weakening their immune system, can be turned around and used to increase the chances of healing and cure.

By taking the energies that are no longer 'running' the patient and using them for positive healing, the chances of recovery are increased. Surgery, chemotherapy and radiation may be tolerated more easily with fewer side effects and the immune system more stimulated to fend off any progression of the disease. Pain and discomfort during these necessary treatments can also cause increased stress. Stress results in increased perception of pain and as pain increases, the stress and fears and worries increase and so sleep becomes restless, disturbed and so pain levels increase once again as the person is worn down in the cycle of fear-stress-pain.

Information and knowledge empowers people and makes them feel better about themselves, more in control. It reduces levels of fear about the unknown and although there is no way we will truly know what happens after death, by exploring possibilities, by encouraging research, discussion, we empower the person facing these issues.

Most patients feel that as long as they can be kept pain free and can sleep well, then they will not be so frightened. Pain is notoriously worse at night as the patient lies in bed awake, and everyone else seems to be asleep. They lie there, wondering what will happen to them, and the fears and resultant stress and pain build.

By facing the fear (**F**alse **E**xpectations **A**ppearing **R**eal) and by giving the patient as much information, education resource material and discussion time as possible, we help to empower them.

Encourage laughter, talking, sharing, pain-reduction techniques and relaxation methods.

For those in palliative care encourage the patient to share with you any unusual incidences, visions or dreams that occur near death. By doing this, you help the person on their journey and the patient may turn out to heal you and your spirit in the process. Children especially are great teachers 'Out of the mouths of babes...'.

Patients need a place to talk about their fears and often medical personnel are not trained to address these issues and have their own issues and taboos around death. We must get through these fears for the sake of our patients. By reading about NDEs, past-life regressions and dying patients' experiences, you can then pass this information on to your other patients.

The spiritual aspect should be addressed and encouraged because it gives so much reassurance to those facing death. This does not have to be the sole responsibility of the Pastor, Priest, Minister, Rabbi or Imam. Many people do not attend church, temple, mosque or synagogue and don't have that resource, or not at the time they need it; for example, in the middle of the night!

Nurses rather than doctors tend to be the most appropriate people to help in the process of dying in the hospital setting. They spend more time with the patient daily. They are there during the long nights when the fear level tends to increase because the distractions of the day are no longer there.

We, the healthcare professions see death more than anyone else. We must stop the silence and start to illuminate and teach the public that death is not the fearsome monster that ignorance and fear create, but can be a gentle release and a gift if fears are addressed and intimacy encouraged. Intimacy of family and friends can be increased as discussion of issues of death and dying occur, allowing more honesty, closeness and vulnerability to replace silence and avoidance of the issue.

The majority of people end up in an acute hospital when they are dying and not in a hospice or at home. I think it is important that all of us in the healthcare system get as comfortable as we can with death and dying issues. If you can't do it, then find someone on your ward who is better at it and let them teach you and show you the way.

Death is *not* a failure; it is a part of living. We can help reduce pain, ease fears and suffering and increase the mental peace, helping the person gather strength for the event and passing. All of this is healing because death is a process, not a failure. We in the helping professions have a responsibility to help our fellows face the inevitable that we all will face eventually.

Our inhibitions about discussing death and its issues arise from a lack of feeling comfortable. We like to *know* how to respond, have the answer at our finger tips and because there is no one answer, format, or pill or fix to dispense, we avoid bringing up the issue. We use 'lack of time' as an excuse to remove ourselves from the patient and any 'difficult, awkward questions they might ask'.

Avoidance is the norm currently because we feel inadequate and are afraid to say the 'wrong' thing. That causes unnecessary suffering mentally and emotionally and probably physically as a result. So I encourage you to be a system breaker and start taking risks.

How often do you go into a patient's room, breeze in cheerfully, open curtains, turn lights on, trot out the phrase 'Good Morning, how are you today?' Do you ask that question with meaning, or is it a habit and you just keep being busy with the chores? Do you really want to hear what they have to say? Do you find that if they start going on and on, you get resentful because you have so much to do today? You make the bed, give medicines, listen to heart sounds, but you are too busy, too rushed, too something to really stop? It is all true, especially today with limited personnel and healthcare costs cutting things down, there is less time to spend listening.

However, you will find that by getting your fear of 'not knowing what to say' out of the way will help you. Allow yourself a few minutes in the room, focusing on the desire and wish to help. Ask the question 'How are you today?' and then pause and wait for the answer. The answer may surprise you and you will know the right thing to do or say. That may be a holding of a hand, getting some water, or allowing words that seem to come from your heart be spoken. The main thing is to release expectations. Don't set yourself up into the mentality of failure. Structure is not always needed; in fact, it can get in the way. I ask you to have the faith and trust that you *can* help, and have the desire to help. Focus on the essence of that, which is love of your fellow man, and act as a channel for the loving care to flow from you to the patient.

'Be Present'. Be fully in the room mentally, physically and spiritually before you begin working. You have no idea at what level you will be able to help. I mention being present – what do I mean by that? I mean when you are with a patient either in an examining cubicle or by a bedside, focus 100% of your attention on the patient. Listen fully, not with half an ear while your mind runs along thinking about your clinic running late, your upcoming surgery, your golf game or your child's problem at school. Focus 100% on the patient for a few minutes and listen to what he or she has to say with no preconceived ideas about what you are going to say or cover – listen with your heart and mind open – pay attention!

I asked a young man what it was like to have lost his mother recently to cancer. Had he felt the staff was as supportive as they could have been? His response was interesting. He told me that both his mother and father had had the same doctor initially. 'My mother did not talk or share with us her dying thoughts, so I don't know how she felt about her doctor. However, after she died, my father changed to another doctor because he felt the doctor was not *listening to him*!'

Sometimes the result may seem insignificant to you, but trust that the process does work, if you focus on being present and desiring to help. You may find yourself saying something to the patient that means nothing to you but it could be of great significance to the patient. For example, you may say something that gives them comfort. It may result in less stress and disease and reduced pain levels, or improved sleep.

You may find yourself drawn to give someone a massage, back rub. Hold their hand. The patient may not have realised that they were hurting in that area but, by your touch, they have been made more at ease, less tense and you have increased their circulation and possibly increased the immune system flow of healing to that area. By releasing your expectations of what should happen when you do 'a, b or c' you don't look for *your edition* of results.

By your words and actions, you may make tremendous improvements to the person's spiritual or mental aspect, even though none is apparent in that moment to their physical condition. You, being clinically trained, look for tangible physical signs and because you may not see them, you immediately doubt yourself and set yourself up as a failure or reject the process.

Yet healing on some level has occurred because you acted with love and care. It is just not yet obvious to you by your standards. It may well manifest later, hours, days, weeks later as the spiritual and or mental healing integrates and then manifests on the physical plane. If we set ourselves up for anticipated results, we will be disappointed and will feel like failures and then we will not expose ourselves again to the experience for fear of failure.

Once we let go of expectations and do the act, with love as our focus, and trust that we will be guided into doing or saying the right thing, we can help in unknown ways. Just by being in the room and giving the space for the patient to talk if they want to, then even silence can be golden. Positive results will happen. They may not come in the form we expected, but only good can come from good intentions.

I have seen births and deaths of babies, I have seen adults, young and old, die. And I have seen how we, as healthcare professionals, do not feel comfortable around discussion of death and dying with the patient. We could talk about the 'the five stages of grief' that Dr Elizabeth Kubler Ross described in her 1969 book 'On Death and Dying'. The feelings of Denial, Anger, Bargaining, Depression, Acceptance and how these stages interweave, come and go and are not usually linear. We are not going to take away the five stages but maybe we can lessen the distress and the length of time it takes to get to the final stage of acceptance. If we can stop seeing death as an ending and see it as a transfer to a level of a new existence, we can begin to release the fear around death and the 'end'.

We can analyse it, we can technically proclaim death's arrival, but when someone looks us in the eye and asks, 'Am I going to die?' How many of us honour that question with honesty? How many of us stammer 'no', avoid the question, pretend it was not asked, leave the room? That person is reaching out to you, asking, and what they are doing takes tremendous courage on their part. There are many who can never get up the courage to even ask the question, or who do not want to know.

How you respond in that moment can make all the difference in the world – theirs and yours. How many of us can sit down, take the person's hand and say, 'Yes, you are and how can I help you face that?'

Those of us who work in palliative care and hospice are experienced with this, but most of us are not. Currently, if we can't 'fix' them, we have 'failed', or the system has, or the right drug has not yet been developed.

What if healing the dying doesn't mean making them well as Western medicine understands it? We can learn how to heal the dying. What is healing? Making whole.

What if healing the dying is simply making the person as whole as they can be body, mind and spirit before they pass on to their next part of the journey of their soul? And surely, we, as caretakers, can help to empower them on this journey into the uncertain future. We can help by supporting them mentally and spiritually as well as physically. We can do this by talking to them and encouraging them to discuss their fears openly. We can guide them to books such as this, hold support groups, make videos of others who are facing their death process; help with laughter, meditation and other alternative or complementary therapies.

The Whole Approach

Take some time; 5 minutes may be all that is needed.

Be open to what may happen.

Ask permission to talk, ask open-ended questions, ask for feedback, being prepared to listen.

Be present – BE in the moment physically, mentally and spiritually, not your body in the room and your mind on something else.

Be trusting – you don't have to know all the answers before you ask the questions; trust that you will know what to say.

Be honest – express your own doubts and fears.

It is OK not to have all the answers. It is OK to say we don't know (which is probably true).

Touch – as appropriate and as needed. Some people are not tactile and may close down if touched. Others crave to be touched. Be your own guide, ask permission, and do what feels right to you in the moment. (It does help if you know what the culturally acceptable thing to do is.)

Let your patient be your guide and teacher. You don't have to know all the answers and be fully prepared. That is so opposite to your training, especially if you are 'co-dependant' as 90% of caregivers are reported to be because we always had to 'know' all the answers, otherwise we'd get caught or punished.

Often the question is asked because the person asking it needs to hear the answer from within, but the act of outwardly voicing the question releases the very information they are seeking.

Patients are people and people are wise. They are not going to let you get away with poor communication. You may think that everything is fine, but patients have feelings, issues and concerns. Often they will not confront you directly, they just silently leave and change their doctor; they go elsewhere, somewhere where they feel heard, cared for as a person, not just a case to be 'fixed.'

When you do start to ask your patient a leading question you may well be amazed at the information you get from someone whom you thought you knew all about.

I found one of my patients had a fear of chemotherapy even more than death and she had resolved that fear after a dream she had of Jesus receiving chemotherapy on her behalf. This dream helped her all through her treatment and her spiritual faith was strengthened by it. I had nursed this lady for over a year and she had not shared this experience with me until I asked her and gave her space to tell me what it was truly like for her to get the diagnosis of breast cancer, and what was her biggest fear. I had never asked her the right question before. She also said that my holding her hand while she was given the diagnosis of breast cancer meant a great deal to her. She said that she felt like a person, rather than a case number or 'just another patient' because she felt the caring through my touch and it was comforting, it made a difference. Subsequently, we felt very connected and I felt enriched and privileged that she had shared such an intimate dream with me. She had shared a part of her 'self" with me, and I felt increased satisfaction with my work. All I had done was to be present, ask a question, and then listen and support her as best as I could.

Life is stressful and we can all get caught up in the rush of work but why are we here and why did we choose to be in the caring professions? Because mostly, we care and we want to enrich ourselves and others, and to show love where we can. If you can feel that, you have made a difference; that is a powerful feeling and one that makes the rest of the day seem easier to get through.

A lady, who lost her son, aged 4 told me, 'My child got the medicine from the doctor, but the care from the nurses. There was one nurse in particular who made herself available, was open, and made me, the mother, feel it was alright to share my confusion, fears and questions. The doctors tried to fix my son, but it was that nurse who was my comforter and supporter. My husband could not face the fact that his son was dying and would not talk about it, and my friends did not know what to say so I found them staying away or feeling awkward. I found myself being artificially bright and reassuring my friends. I was outwardly very 'together', but at night I fell apart and felt so alone with no one to turn to. Finally, I was actually telling a friend how badly my son was doing and she said, "Gosh, it sounds like you don't care," and that hurt me very much'.

You may say that these are things that should be dealt with by the person's Minister, but nowadays a lot of people do not go to church or religious centres of worship. They may have issues about God, religion, dogma etc., so they may not want to talk to a Minister, Priest, Rabbi or Imam. So they may be much more inclined to talk to you, their doctor or nurse, especially if they are spending long hours in hospital.

People are very different in how they respond to any situation. The lady who lost her son still finds it very difficult to talk to people about death, despite her experience. Her mother-in-law has cancer and goes to a support group at an oncology centre, where there is a meditation garden, library, counselling, hugs and laughter therapy. She loves it and looks forward to her sessions. Conversely, this same lady has a friend who has been diagnosed with breast cancer and who has chosen to shut herself up in her house and shut herself off from support. There is no 'right' way for all people, but there are plenty of people who want help and support but don't know how to ask for it.

So I would encourage you that when you go in to see your patient, instead of just doing a medical check, or a 'vitals' round, make a conscious connection with your patient and check on his or her whole being, mental and spiritual as well as physical well-being.

Ask permission and give a back or neck rub, or hold a hand and make a true connection. You will be enriched by the experience as they will be, more often than not.

I know of an oncology nurse who, when asked to put up in her treatment room a poster talking about the joy of living for today (for that is what we each have in the moment the here and now), she declined. Her response was 'no' because she saw it as a negative focus and not a positive one. She did not want anything 'negative in my treatment room'. She saw discussion of possible death as a negative and so wished to avoid anything that might stir up questions. Yet she had all these patients sitting or lying there receiving chemotherapy for their life-threatening illness, probably each of them wondering why and what if. Yet she did not want it to be a consideration. I think she was not addressing her patients' needs because she could not look at her own issues around death.

I would like to see healthcare teams created who can spend more time with patients, not just terminal patients but for anyone that needs some support that will take time.

Until your hospital gets such a team, you can be the one to take a few minutes, make a few minutes to stop, be present, say hallo and ask, 'How are you doing? Can I help in any way' and wait for the patient to talk.

Don't limit this approach to just patients who are dying. Use the whole approach for all your patients, the recent heart attack, the stroke victim, the asthmatic, the chronic illness patients. They all have had life-threatening events and have their fears.

One person can make a difference – why not let it be you. You are good enough and you will know exactly what will be the right thing to say and do, when you come from the intention of love and caring. Connect with your essence, your caring and your desire to help others. Go be a healer and a comforter.

We need to be willing to be the 'single light' that goes forth to meet and 'light the next candle'. The light of information will gradually spread and as with the ripple effect of water, or the 100th monkey phenomena occurs, the world will gradually become more enlightened about death and dying and it can all start with you. *You can make a difference.*

We can make the choice to help to make a difference and we do not need to be an expert with a degree, doctorate or specialist in dying. We have life experience, we work alongside death frequently. We are privileged by having seen dying and death, and how peaceful it can be. We as healthcare workers have seen more death than most people and yet we feel limited in our knowledge. But we are experts through our familiarity.

We can choose when next asked, 'Am I going to die?' to stop and say 'Would you like to talk? I can spend some time with you now', or 'I can't stop right now but I would like to come back and discuss it with you later', or you can call someone on the healing team to come and talk.

If the patient is asking the question, they want to know the truthful answer. It takes courage to ask the question. Don't brush it aside with a platitude. They have asked you because they feel an affinity with you, they trust you and feel close to you. They are being vulnerable and it is a major question for them. Please don't turn your back on them because of your own fears. Acknowledge you have heard the question and that you will talk with them or will get someone who can.

Equally remember that some people don't want to know they are dying, or have cancer, so you must respect how they want things handled. Trust me, you will know those who want to talk, to discuss, and those that do not.

We are not and will never be ready for that question unless we face our own fears and become conversant with the many aspects of death and its possibilities.

I would like to see hospitals have on their staff, a counsellor or nurse specialist who is comfortable with discussing death and dying. This person would be in attendance when the doctor or surgeon gives the diagnosis. The patient could then meet or have a phone call with this specialist again to discuss their various issues. They would have the time that the doctors often do not have to spend with the patient. Obviously, the medical questions would be handled by the doctor directly.

All through life, we meet people who teach us formally and informally about life. Let your patient be your teacher at times; you may learn something. For the patient's sake, I encourage you to stretch a little, do a little risk taking. Stop limiting yourself and allow yourself to come out of your comfort zone.

Please don't abandon your patient at the very time he or she needs you the most. You may well be a patient sometime, so put yourself in the patient's position and walk a mile in their shoes.

I think you will find it more rewarding, heartwarming and hopefully give you an increased feeling of work satisfaction.

Chapter 6

Life, Death and Life after Death

What do we really know about life, death and the afterlife? Not a lot.

In fact, about life after death, we know nothing 100% for sure. We are born, we gasp, breathe, grow, live, learn and then we die.

We each travel a similar yet different path of growing up, school, learning, living, loving, having children, retiring, growing older and then getting ready for the next phase… death.

We go along the path of life, some of us knowing what we are here for and doing it.

Most of us stumble along as best we can, facing difficulties as they occur, and we live our lives without too many questions. 'Life happens while we are busy making plans'.

But what of life and death, and life after death? Why don't we talk about these issues more?

Because, in the Western world especially, it is not acceptable culturally to talk about death; there tends to be a taboo about it. So a lot of us go through life never thinking or talking about death until we are staring it in the face. When we do talk about it, it is usually because a loved one is facing death or has just died, or possibly our own end is looming up as a reality.

Stories of life after death are anecdotal in our society, experiential and written about more frequently recently, since resuscitation techniques have developed and improved. People who 20 years ago would have died due to car accidents, heart attacks etc. are returning from the 'jaws' of death to recount their experiences. Scientists will talk of oxygen deprivation, affecting certain brain areas causing visual and auditory hallucinations. However, the anecdotal tales all over the world are very similar. They report seeing family members, who have already died, feelings of love, joy and peace. Children who have had near-death experiences (NDEs); on seeing photos of relatives who died before the child was born; tell you that they met those people while they were experiencing their 'going-into-the-light' journey. These experiences are called NDEs.

Some patients report seeing a special loved one at the end of the bed as they are dying. My mother saw my father at the end of her bed in her last two days. I asked her if she saw him and she indicated yes. So I told her that he had come to take her home and that it was fine for her to let go. That I would manage fine by myself as she had a good job of bringing me up.

We walk around on this Earth as physical bodies, made up of bones, muscles, skin and liquid. We have various large organs inside us, we have various shades of coloured hair and skin and different appearances, but for all intents and purposes, we walk around on this planet as bodies and that is who we are...or are we more than that?

We are so much more than just our bodies; we consist of body, mind and spirit. As someone once said to me, 'We are spiritual beings living in human form' and I believe they were right. We tend, during our lifetime, to forget that. We distance ourselves unwittingly from our Source, or spiritual base and society encourages that separation.

We have children playing with their 'invisible friends' and they talk of being here before or of being 'big before.' For a few years, we let them talk like this, laughing at the comments. Then around the age of five or six, we start to discourage them. It is not considered the 'normal' thing to do or socially acceptable in *this* society. However, in other cultures, reincarnation and spirit realms are very much the normal accepted belief.

A friend of mine was telling her four-year-old son off for doing something wrong. He turned around and said, 'It didn't used to be like this; I used to be the one telling you off when I was big!'

Another friend's child would talk quite happily of having been to this planet four or five times before, until at the age of 7, when he began to get self-conscious of his 'different' kind of comments and he would clam up when asked specific questions. Left alone to be spontaneous he would continue to make unusual comments. He informed his mother one day that he had been given the choice of three sets of parents and he had chosen her and his dad because they needed him the most! This certainly surprised her, but we do arrive on Earth as babies and what are babies? Some say they are angels, some say spirits embodied, but they are certainly flesh and blood. They arrive as little solid packages, howling, crying, hungry, and we love them, feed them, clothe them and treat them as human beings.

As a trainee midwife, in my early 20s, I worked the nightshift on several occasions. One of my duties was in the nursery, where I would feed the babies during the night so the mothers could get some sleep. My nights were filled with feeding babies with bottles of formula every three to four hours and changing their diapers (nappies) as they needed. I had lots of time to observe these babies, some of them less than 24 hours old, some as 'old' as six days.

It fascinated me that they were all so different from each other and I don't mean by their appearance, height, weight and colourings. They each had distinct personalities and response to life. How was it that they were so different in behaviour? They had not had time to imprint from their parents' behaviour, so what was causing this? I also noted that some of them appeared to be 'new' as if this was their first time here; yet others had an air of wisdom or age to them, like an 'old soul'. These 'old-soul' babies would stare at me with wisdom in their eyes that was way beyond their few hours of age. My only explanation is that part of us is our spirit that we have carried on from before, and we bring our consciousness, our knowing, with us as we arrive on this planet.

Another example that shows us we are more than just bodies, are psychics and mediums. If you have ever gone to see a good one, I'm sure you were amazed at the information that the psychic had about you. Some use their tools of the trade, tarot cards, crystal balls and astrological charts, but others go way beyond these tools, and tap into a greater knowing or the area of 'Collective Unconscious', attaining information that is not within the realms of their 'tools'. They are the intermediaries who can communicate with our loved ones who have already died, and can give messages from our spirit friends. These different examples show us that we are more than just a physical being, born onto this planet to grow, mature, develop and then die.

We are powerful spiritual beings that choose to come to this planet to learn, grow and evolve, and it takes courage to be here, for life on this planet is not easy.

I believe we each choose to come to this planet we call Earth, in order to accomplish a task, a mission and to achieve spiritual progress along the way. Our goal is to complete that task before we leave and return to the spirit realm from whence we came.

Our goal is also to become better beings as we walk this path and live this life. Just because you die doesn't make you good because you are in spirit form. If you were a 'bad guy' in this life, you will not transform into a 'good guy' by dying. You are still you, you take the essence that was you, leaving your physical body behind, like a snake shedding its skin.

Contrary to appearance, we are not just material. We are energy and we will always exist, in some energetic form. According to people who have had NDEs you get to review your actions in the life you have just had and see how your actions affected others, family, friends, etc. You also get to see if you accomplished your mission, or the task that you chose to do while on Earth. Whether you evolved or regressed on your path of spiritual growth. You are the judge and jury of your life.

We have probably lived many lifetimes already, many reincarnations through time that have assisted us in our growth and evolution along the path of enlightenment. It is through these episodes that you, your soul, essence, spirit, have gained enlightenment at many different levels. Different lessons have been sought, taught and gained mastery over. These lessons have been your markers, your growth times, your question times, your asking times, your seeking times, your trial times, your dark times, your pain times, your crying times. These are all lessons that you have chosen to go through in order to become a wiser, softer, gentler, kinder person. The lessons give you new perspectives, new insights, inner growth and increased knowledge about life, yourself and others.

Realise that when you have a difficult lesson, that it is a gift to you and others. It allows a time for adversity and subsequent reflection, inner consideration and contemplation.

Often, adversity is actually an opportunity; like feeling fear can be a form of excitement.

Lessons often involve other people which allows their own lessons to unfold for them.

So we can also be a catalyst for other people's growth.

Freedom of choice is a right given to you at birth to use as you will.

It is in the choosing of your path on this planet that helps you to learn a particular lesson.

Perhaps I need to start by telling you of my experience with reincarnation. A school girl friend took me along to meet her mother when I was 16 and the mother talked to me about her beliefs and for the first time, life and death started to make sense. I had always thought what a waste of human life and potential if we go through all the trials and struggles of our own life, only to end up as nothing. All the learning through life, lost. Then what was life all about? It did not make sense to me that we would grow, learn, struggle and then die and not somehow continue on after all that we had learnt.

My friend's mother's thoughts made sense. I felt my 'ah ha, this feels right' response when she talked to me of her beliefs about reincarnation.

Reincarnation involves the belief that people are born, grow, learn, die, stay in spiritual form for a period of time and then may choose to reincarnate again as physical beings. This repeats in cycles, the soul continuing to learn and evolve along their spiritual growth until they become so 'enlightened' that they have no need to keep returning to learn more on this planet. The belief is that although you can stay in spirit form and progress, more is learnt by becoming 'embodied' as a physical being. The spirit decides on the lesson or lessons they most need to learn at the time and then chooses the type of life pattern that would help them most. So when we see children born into horrible conditions or with handicaps, rather than wondering if there is a God. Realise that this spirit probably chose a condition to mostly help them develop spiritually.

As the saying goes, 'Walk a mile in my shoes to really understand my life'.

The belief also is that families tend to reincarnate together in a close time frame to continue lessons together. So a couple may be reborn as brother and sister, or mother and child. Also, friends tend to reincarnate together around the same time but may not meet up on the physical plane for several years.

There are also beliefs that people who are killed suddenly will tend to reincarnate more quickly than others, maybe within a few years of death, to allow them to fulfil their lesson. I met a man who was convinced that he knew me in 1942 in France. (I was born in 1952.) However I was able to speak French when I was three to five years old because I had a French-speaking Lebanese nanny. But I also dreamed of German soldiers in a camp when I was seven to eight years old for some reason. This man was a neighbour, 30 years older than me who had been in the French Resistance during World War II. He said I had been a Jewish French girl who was captured and killed in 1942. I am not able to explain this but he was a well-respected Professor of French at a UK University. There are those who believe that we choose all the main events of our life, including when and how we die. The saying 'there are no accidents' is a well-known fatalistic belief.

The belief is that when we die, our real self leaves the body and travels into another dimension, sometimes through a tunnel, or towards a bright light, with guardian helpers or with other 'transferring' spirits. When we arrive at the other side, we evaluate our most recent life, judge ourselves and our actions, and then rest for a while. The time of rest depends on how tired or sick we were in the physical world. If we suddenly died in an accident, we may need time to readjust to the fact that we are in fact no longer living a human life.

There is a belief that those who commit suicide pause their spiritual growth. This is because they were unable to face or deal with their chosen life lesson, so they opted out. They tend to return again later to learn their lesson. To take one's life before it is really time is a shame because it is a rejection of the gift of human life that was given to you by God.

Do you believe in reincarnation? Our belief about death and reincarnation usually stems from our families and their religious beliefs. The belief in reincarnation was held by the majority of religions in the past.

The Western world, which, being predominately Christian, does not believe in reincarnation due to the historical banishment in the Bible. The early Christians believed in reincarnation and there used to be many references to the subject in the early bible. However, the leaders of the Church in A.D. 553 held 'The Second Council of Constantinople' and removed most references to reincarnation. The reason apparently was that the Church wanted total control over its members, and they felt that if people thought that they'd get other chances to 'get it right', that there would not be enough control. So the policy of hellfire and damnation and a wrathful God was implemented.

Preaching began to talk of mortal sins staining your soul and of being condemned to Hell.

An unloving, unforgiving judgmental God and a place called Purgatory. There were fear-based teachings to get your money, gifts and keep control of wealth and property.

If you did not worship the way the Church wanted you to, then you were punished, tortured, killed in the name of God during Inquisitions. Popes would give blessings and forgiveness to the Inquisitors as they were deemed to be doing God's work! Very often, it was over gaining land and power from others, such as the Cathars in Europe.

I have never understood why God was pictured by some religions as being so harsh, rigid and unforgiving. That wasn't the picture drawn by the teachings of Jesus as far as I could tell. How could un-baptised children be condemned to

Purgatory or Limbo? That did not match with the 'suffer little children to come unto me' image.

Many Eastern religions still believe in reincarnation and in fact celebrate death as a progression, particularly Hindu, Buddhist and Moslem amongst others.

The 'ancestors' are revered, consulted and respected. Old souls who reincarnate are respected. The Dalai Lama is chosen based on the belief of a person reincarnating. Children talking about past lives are encouraged, not disbelieved.

When death occurs, there is celebration that the soul has gone back to spirit form to be with God and funeral attendees wear red or white, not the black of mourning.

Some people believe that this life that we are living right now is the 'hell' and the trial and the test. That to die is a blessed event because for now the lesson is over and the person can be with God again.

There are people going to specialists for past-life regressions. Hypnotherapists have found that some people under hypnosis have spontaneously reverted to another life they have experienced. Usually one that has a pertinent lesson in it for use in the current life. Clients have been led back into memories of being in the womb of this life, returning to spirit and regressing back further to another life. They do this in order to learn why certain themes, trends or events in this life may be occurring.

Usually, it is just glimpses of a life, a piece of it, a sense or theme. The therapist will ask the person once they have experienced the life and maybe received the awareness they are looking for, to go to the end of that life and as they view their dying, see what is the lesson they believe they learnt in that lifetime.

For a traumatic death, they can 'view' it removed from the emotion. The information can then be brought to this life, and that wisdom can hopefully bring awareness and understanding to present day problems. Awareness of an issue is a good step towards resolution.

For example, awareness of being an alcoholic is a big step towards curing the problem; and certainly the first step. So if someone has an irrational fear of flying, for example, and then learns through past-life regression that they died as a pilot in a war, that knowledge gives the person a basis on which they can work out their fear of flying, knowing that it is not a fear based on *this* life.

My mother had an irrational fear of snakes, including even seeing them in a magazine, when she would scream and throw the magazine across the room, much to the surprise of my father!

Many therapists are using Past Life Regression to help people with phobias as well as other stresses in their lives. Some people who have haunting dreams of past lives are also being helped by this therapy. Some are just doing it to find out why they have a special interest in say Egyptian History versus Indian. Maybe because they lived an Egyptian life at some time, but never incarnated as an Indian!

NDEs are a fairly new phenomenon. With the advent of resuscitation techniques and the continuing developing improvement of this science, more and more of us are surviving events that normally we would not have, we are being 'saved' and are continuing on with our life. These people who have experienced NDE have a common story of separation of spirit from body, a drifting above the body. Then they feel they are traveling towards a white warm light, sometimes passing through a tunnel, with or without a guide. They usually meeting someone they knew, who has already died. A review of life may occur, or a journeying to an area of learning. They are told it is not their time yet and they need to return to Earth as they still have things to do.

Or if given the choice, the person decides to return because of someone else, possibly a young child who would be left alone. Most say that given the choice they would rather have stayed on the other side because of the love and beauty that was there.

The common theme that they all share is that on their return to this life, they have a different perspective about life. There is often a character change, with an increased awareness and caring for others. A wider interest in the world as a whole, a less self-centred focus, and a desire to help their fellow man and to have a meaningful life.

Also, they seem to lose any fear they had about death and look forward to the time when it will be the right time for them to pass over. They all agree that their experience has had a profound effect on them, and these stories have a similarity the world over.

As a nurse, I have sometimes asked patients if they have had an experience after they have survived a 'code blue' or resuscitation. Most patients will not volunteer the experiences they have had because they are afraid that they will be thought of as crazy or of imagining things. However, if directly asked specific questions, they will share their experience. I had a patient tell me he had floated out of his body, up to the ceiling. He had looked down and seen the 'code team' working on his body. He could hear what they were saying and witness their actions with a sense of detachment, neither wishing them to succeed or not succeed. Then two entities were suddenly beside him and they felt like very old friends to him. They guided him away from the room and into a bright warm-lighted area. He had the sense of moving fast with other beings as well as his two companions along a corridor or tunnel of white warmth towards a brighter light. He said he had no sense of fear; in fact, everything felt right and comfortable. Then he was aware that the movement forward stopped and in fact, he was beginning to move backwards. He said he was aware that it was 'not his time yet' and then he found himself back in his body, opening his eyes and seeing the doctors and nurses around him who had successfully resuscitated him. He told me he had felt very confused and had mixed emotions about being back in his body as the sensation of peace and love and rightness had been so nice while he was out of his body. He was aware that it was not yet his time to die, and he hoped that he could make his life have more meaning for himself and others in the future.

Another lady I knew had 'died', following difficulty with breathing. She was already in the hospital having been hit by a car. She felt herself leave her body and float above it towards a light that she was attracted to. As she was beginning to enter this light, she noticed a very tall being beside her, strong wise, possibly male. They communicated by thought, and together they went into this tunnel of light. She was not aware of others around her but as soon as she got through the tunnel she started to look for her oldest son who had died two years earlier. She was not able to find him immediately and she then felt that she was being given a choice of either staying or returning to Earth. On the one hand, she wanted to stay, find her son, and be in the atmosphere of peace and joy that she was feeling. However, she had another son who was 11 years old, living back on Earth and not wanting to leave him to grow up without her, she decided to return to Earth. She was not aware of any trip back, just that as soon as she made up her mind, she found herself back in her body, with a breathing tube in her throat, having been intubated during the resuscitation. She was depressed and sad at being back in her body and it took her a few days to come to terms with the fact that she was back in her body, as she was in a lot of pain from the accident that she had been in. She was also sad that she had not seen her older son during her NDE. She realised after a time that had she seen him, she would not have been able to leave him to return to be with her younger son who needed her. So by not seeing her older son, she was able to freely make the choice to return to Earth.

When I met her, it was three weeks since this had happened and she was still quite torn at the decision she had made. Although she knew she had made the right decision, she wished that she had stayed in spirit, because of the deep peace and love she had felt there. She also was wishing she had had the presence of mind to ask the guide all sorts of questions, but felt everything had happened so fast.

I suggested to her that she had been given a gift of being made aware of her guide and that by focusing on the memory, she might be able to recall him/her and be able to communicate with her guide through dreams or meditation.

It is thought that the energies that come to meet you to travel with you through the light may be your guardian angels or spirits that have been around you during your life, to help you when needed. These may well be the 'imaginary friends' that young children see and play with. The belief is that they are always around but cannot communicate with you until you seek them out. They cannot give you answers until you ask the questions.

The Bible saying, 'Seek and ye will find, knock and it shall be opened to you' takes on a new meaning in this context.

I had a surprise once when I was driving on a freeway and started to move into the fast lane. My steering wheel was literarily moved sharply back in the other direction with an energy that took me totally by surprise. At the same instance, a car that I had not seen, passed me by in the lane that I was about to have driven into. Without a doubt, there would have been a horrible crash, which I would have caused. The interesting thing was, as the steering wheel was taken out of my control and moved, I heard this voice say 'Pay attention'. This was not my own self-talk. I truly believe that my own guardian angel saved me from an accident and possible death, while telling me off at the same time!

Children have a gift of total acceptance, love and being open until we re-educate them and train them that it is not always so safe to do so. They have a simplicity that shows itself by the way they speak spontaneously about things. When corrected or questioned they tend to clam up, thinking they have done something wrong. Their spontaneous comments give us an insight into life before life, or life after death. They are nearer in years to the 'veil of forgetfulness' and so maybe the veil is more transparent for them and they are able to remember more clearly than we as adults are.

Children also have their tales of NDEs, and they have clarity about oncoming death. They have a level of acceptance and less fear than adults around their dying. They have much more concern about the grief and sadness that their parents, siblings and friends are going through. This peace and acceptance of their demise may well come from the fact that as they have so recently arrived from the spirit realm, that they remember, and possibly welcome the release. There are people who believe that each infant has the choice of whether or not they will stay on this planet once they are born. Some explanation of crib death is the choice that these little souls make to return to spirit. They have the choice until around one year of age, when they have to decide whether they are staying or leaving. The use of apnoea mattresses on infants that have a tendency to stop breathing while sleeping are usually needed only in the first year of life. Apnoea rarely occurs beyond one year of age. There is an interesting story of a baby that kept having apnoea episodes and the parents used an apnoea mattress constantly until the baby's first birthday. The mattress was removed and the baby died a few nights later; coincidence?

There is a lovely story I heard recently of a five year old going into his baby brother's room and, unaware that he was being watched by his mother, whispered into his brother's ear, "Tell me what God is like; I've almost forgotten."

Chapter 7

Getting Ready to Say Goodbye Soon or Aged 100+

This is the practical chapter, the 'to-do' list for those of you who have been given a time span for your death, or for those of you who are wise enough to realise that death and dying are a state of life and certain affairs run more smoothly if pre-arranged. I also would encourage everyone to write a Living Will/Advanced Directive and a Will from an early age because you never know if you may suddenly be involved in an accident and be in a coma permanently or have a heart attack and die on the spot. I wrote my first Will at age 26 and I revise it periodically...being prepared!

You might need to have others help you legally manage your financial affairs and healthcare issues if you become severely unwell. You can have Power of Attorney papers drawn up specifying who you want. You can have different people for your financial affairs and your healthcare. Please remember that you must sign these while you are still considered to be of 'sound mind'. The documents are registered but not necessarily activated until you are ready.

The reason I am including this chapter is based largely on my personal life. I had very little interaction with death on a personal level. I had seen death many times in hospitals, but my exposure to it was limited to delivering the body to the morgue of the hospital. What happened beyond that was a bit of a mystery to me. Coming from a small family and being overseas when my grandparents died, meant that what had to be done after the event was something others had dealt with, but never me. However, several years ago, my father died and within 24 hours, I had flown home from America to Scotland to help my mother. My best friend met me at the train station and driving me home advised me that she had been to the registrar's office to register my father's death. However, she had not had the right papers with her and would have to return the next day with them. It dawned on me that not only was I going to be the sole support for my mother over the next few weeks, but that there were a series of affairs that had to be dealt with, and I did not have the slightest idea about what I needed to know. The funeral director was helpful to an extent but a lot of things I found out by trial, error and general guesswork. The hard thing about this is that right when you are in the middle of trying to cope with the death and loss of a loved one, and the shock and numbness is present, you are expected to try and deal with bureaucracy and think practically. That is very hard to do when your partner, parent, child, loved one has just died. You can cope and manage but it is easier to have a checklist to refer to and the input and preparation, done by the person who has just died is invaluable if at all possible.

My uncle, two months after my father had died, asked me what hints or tips I would give to him, or what thing I had learnt from this experience. I told him that the thing that would have helped me the most would have been a checklist of things that needed to be done in the event of someone close to me dying. He said 'Well I have this book that tells me what to do'. He produced a thick heavy book. I explained that a big detailed book is helpful if you are in the state of mind to either read it ahead of time or have time to ponder through it. The first few days after someone dies, all you can do is the things that are directly in front of you; you cope and that is about it. So here are my suggestions and checklists and I hope that this helps you.

Wills and Trusts

Consult the experts regarding your financial affairs. Minimise your death duties and taxes exposure, by using all legal means possible. Don't let the tax man have monies that your family could have had with a little forethought and tax and estate planning. Due to a family experience, I decided to put a clause in my will that stated if anyone challenged my will, they would receive nothing. The main thing is to keep it legal.

Make lists of all your bank accounts, the phone numbers, account numbers, stocks and shares. A summary of the amounts, updated every so often is also helpful because sometimes there is an expectation that there is more money than there actually is. Then time and worry go into trying to 'find it', when it was never there in the first place.

We all think we are organised or know we should be, but most of us are not!

My uncle asked me to be an executor of his will. He told me 'It will be really easy, just one phone-call to my lawyer and she will handle everything' WRONG! It turned out that she had details about his will but that was all. My dear uncle's financial statements were scattered, everywhere. There were little notes with initials and amounts. My cousin and I had to figure out which initials were for which bank, building society or investments, stocks etc. It was a nightmare of organising, phone calls, letters, stopping direct debits, mail transfers that went on for several months.

So please, make it easy for your loved ones and executors of your will. Have a written document with your financial affairs listed as best you can with as much detail as possible.

If you live alone, list all your information and wishes, sign and date it. Make copies and send it to relatives stating where they will find your will, papers, which funeral home, which lawyer you use etc. You know it all but do not assume that others will know. Make it as smooth sailing for them as possible!

Give them a chance to have space and a place to say their 'official' goodbyes to you. My father was not a church attendee or believer and so a service in the church was not held. The nearest crematorium was a two-hour drive away. Many friends could not do that trip, so they didn't get a chance to 'officially' say goodbye. They did let the family know later, when it was too late, that they felt they had missed out on being able to formally say goodbye. So when you plan how you want to be remembered, remember others and think what they would also like. My dear friend, who died years ago, was not a practicing Catholic. So no church service was held, but there was a memorial service at his place of work where his work colleagues were able to say goodbye and got up to speak about him. Then there was an all-day party held at his home to celebrate his life. There was so much Spirit, God and love in those two areas that it was amazing. Two different yet beautiful ways of saying goodbye, remembering good times, saying caring and supportive things to others who also were grieving.

So you see, it does not have to be a religious affair, unless you wish it. Think about these things and plan for them. They will happen and you might as well have a say in your affairs!

Be smart. Get organised. Living wills, Estate planning, Wills and Trusts. How you would like to die, heroic measures or 'no code – do not resuscitate'. After death, do you want to be an organ donor; buried or cremated? Church service or home party? Have you listed your financial affairs, bank accounts etc.?

Information List for Your Nearest and Dearest

The reason for this is sound. You know a lot of information about yourself that others do not and this will help them. Leave this with your solicitor or executor of your will, with a copy of it in a safe place, easily found by your family.

- Your name and address, your date of birth and place of birth
- Your father's full name and his occupation, date of birth, address, and date and place where he died
- Your mother's full name including her maiden name before she married, her address and date of birth
- Name of your spouse/partner and any former spouse or deceased spouse
- Ideally have their birth, death certificates or marriage certificates, or copies
- Names and date of birth of any children
- Your Social Security Number [USA] or National Insurance Number [UK] or whatever is your national ID number
- Your National Health Number [UK] and/or Your Medical Record Number (UK/USA)
- Your main doctor's name, address, phone number and email address
- Where your will is located: Is it with your solicitor/attorney or in a bank or a house file?
- Lawyer or solicitor's name address, phone number and email address
- If you are a sole parent, who will become the guardian of your children?

- Where are your important keys to be found: Safe, car, desk, house, etc.
- What arrangements do you have for any pets?
- Do you have a Life Insurance Policy with account number?
- Do you have a prepaid funeral plan? Have you bought a burial plot?

List where to find things such as:

- Birth Certificates
- Marriage Certificates
- Insurance Policies
- Stocks and Shares Certificates
- Title Deeds of House
- Lease of Property Agreements
- Bank Accounts
- National Savings Accounts
- Building Society Account Books
- Pension Documents
- Income Tax Papers
- Receipts
- Burial Plot Papers
- Car Log Book and Insurance Certificates
- Computer Access Codes and Passwords List

Your Financial Details

List all your bank accounts, credit unions, stocks, shares, mutual funds, building societies, premium bonds (UK) or any place you have invested monies. List the company names, addresses, phone numbers, emails and account numbers.

Periodically update these and having an approximate value of each listed is helpful. Many thousands of pounds and dollars are lying in unclaimed bank accounts because no one knew they were there!

If you have a lawyer, financial advisor or tax accountant, list their names, address and phone number. It is important to remember that all your accounts will be frozen on notification of your death and your spouse/partner will not be able to access monies from these sources unless you have a shared bank account. Release of monies to relatives and friends occurs after wills or probate affairs are completed. This can take anywhere from two months to a couple of years to accomplish depending on how straightforward your affairs are. If you want to provide for a partner immediately after your death, I would suggest that you consider giving them monies before you die; or have a significant sum of money in your shared account.

When a close friend died, his distant family were convinced there where gold bars hidden in some account, or under the bed! There was not, but it caused them upset and concern until satisfied that there were no 'forgotten accounts'.

Funeral Arrangements

What type of funeral would you like? Burial or cremation, nature, church or humanist service? What hymns, prayers, poems, verses would you like at your service? Provide a copy of these with your Will so your friends don't have to search for them.

Have you got a prepaid funeral plan arranged or will your estate or benefactors pay?

What religion are you? Where is the religious service to be held at?

Who would you like to officiate at the service?

Do you own a burial plot? What is the plot number? Is there a family churchyard where you want to be buried?

Who should hold the cords to lower your coffin into the ground? This is usually considered an honour because they would be people especially close to you.

If you want to be cremated, where do you want your ashes scattered or do you want them kept in an Urn? I have a friend who keeps the ashes of all her past pets. She wants them buried with her when she dies. Who would know this unless she writes it down?

Is the final ceremony to be a funeral, a memorial or a celebration of your life? Is it to be private and limited to family? Are flowers to be sent, from family only or from anyone? And what happens to them afterwards? I personally would prefer flowers from my garden, or plants that can be planted afterwards as a permanent memorial. Or would you rather have donations given to charities? If so, list your preferred charities.

Is there going to be a reception afterwards? If so, where and what will be served. Often that depends on the time of the funeral service. Tea, coffee, alcohol, lunch, party? Do you want a memorial book signed?

Do you have any preference for the inscription on your memorial headstone or urn?

If you are being cremated, what is to happen to your ashes?

Before the Funeral

Make a list for close relatives, asking them to inform the following people and include their addresses, phone numbers and email addresses:

- Relatives and friends who you would like to attend if possible
- Solicitor and executors
- Funeral director or undertaker
- Minister/Priest/Rabbi/Imam, etc.
- Registrar of births, deaths and marriages

Death Announcement: What newspaper and what type of announcement? Write out a sample if you like. A notice of this is usually posted in the window of the undertaker in the United Kingdom and that is how local friends and neighbours learn when the funeral is.

What clubs, trade unions or professional organisations should be informed?

After the Funeral

Someone, usually the executor needs to instruct the solicitor/lawyer to wind up the estate unless you feel able to handle it yourself. This can normally wait a couple of months while necessary papers arrive.

Make claims under the following insurance policies: Life, accident and any others. Include the company name, address, phone number, email and policy numbers.

Notify the employment company and see if you qualify for part of a retirement pension, or forces pensions, or government pensions.

Inform Inspector of Taxes: Include Tax ID number (Social Security Number (USA) or National Insurance Number (UK)).

Claim social security benefits: Widows benefit, industrial death, if applicable.

In the United Kingdom, some local councils will give you a council rate discount for living alone. In Scotland, it is currently a 25% discount.

If necessary, inform various companies: Gas, electricity, telephone, milkman, newsagent, postal services.

Return driver's license, passport and Social Security Card (USA) to appropriate authorities.

Carry out instructions about any pets.

Check for any assets or liabilities and where to find documents on bank loans, mortgages, loan agreements, credit card information.

Phew! You did not know there was so much to know about you, did you?

Remember all of the above notations are helpful to your family and friends for when you have gone and they are trying to get things organised. My mother was asked three days after her mother died what hymns she would like at the funeral service and she couldn't think of one! In the first few weeks after death, relatives cope and manage, but the shock and numbness precludes proper clear thinking and that is why a checklist is so helpful. Please remember that this checklist is not a will and you need to make one, otherwise your wishes may not be met.

I found that the time around the death and until the funeral was very busy with phone calls and many arrangements to be made. After the funeral, there is nothing really to be done for a month or two. Then things got busy again as legal papers arrive and paperwork started around closing the estate.

This is a long to-do list. Take it bit by bit over several days. Remember that you can revise it, adjust it anytime. It does not have to be 'perfect'. Just do as much as you can.

Keep refreshing the details from time to time as life changes occur. Particularly if you travel a lot, live far away from your family, which so many of us do nowadays.

You also always have the choice. To do all this, or choose not to do any of it and not even discuss the issues. Your life and the way you die is truly in your hands.

So you are really doing your family and friends a huge favour by getting your affairs in order, whether you die soon or when you are 100+!

Remember also that how you die will impact those left behind. Your organised peaceful death will help those you love.

Be Prepared

And no, doing this stuff is not being negative and will not bring your death sooner!

Chapter 8

Terminal Time – Are You Ready to Go?

'I'm sorry to have to tell you that despite our best efforts, there is now nothing more we can do for you. I am going to transfer your case to the palliative care team who will take over your care from here. I suggest that you get your affairs in order as you have only a short time remaining'.

Hopefully, you will be told this openly and honestly at the point in time when the doctors have decided that you are 'terminal'. No further medical treatment can be done to help you recover

Nowadays, we are much better at taking care of the dying patient and their family and friends. Palliative care and hospice workers are specialists in caring for the dying. There is usually a great support system once the patient is diagnosed as 'terminal'. I am not going to go into much discussion about these areas as they are already well covered and lots of information is available.

However, it can sometimes take a while for that terminal diagnosis to be made, so it is important for all of us, the patient, relatives and healthcare staff to be proactive, informed and open minded.

'Am I treating this person as I would like to be treated if it was me?' is a great mental reference point to start from. 'There but for the grace of God go I'.

So you have been told that there is nothing more that Western medicine can do for you. You have been through the mill with tests, drugs, surgery, chemotherapy and/or radiation. You have had highs and lows, worries and fears and now your main fear has been realised.

You have been diagnosed as terminal and been given a period of time to get your affairs in order. Hopefully, you have been thinking about these issues already.

You have arrived at the departure lounge of life and you would be wise to think about what 'route' you want to take. I don't mean to sound facetious but there are things to discuss and issues to look at.

Medical and Nursing Support

Pain medication if needed should be supplied liberally so the patient can be pain-free if at all possible. Being calm and peaceful but not heavily sedated. You, the patient, don't want to feel confused or too drowsy or 'out of control'. A patient-controlled analgesia machine may be ideal in these circumstances because then you, the patient is in control, and you cannot overdose on the medication.

At this point, I want to say to those of us who worry about addiction and overuse of narcotics, stop worrying about it for the terminally ill patient. 'So what' if they become addicted. The person is about to die and if they can die peacefully and not in pain, calm instead of restless, content instead of fearful; then we are doing them a service and a kindness. We tend to get so caught up in the 'It hasn't been 4 hours since your last shot' scenario. Rather than judging the patient for being too demanding, or drug dependent; if we see that our patient is uncomfortable we should become active advocates. Don't complain to your colleagues that 'Mrs Smith is always asking for pain medication'. Or try to be the judge and jury and tell the patient that he 'shouldn't be having this much pain'. How do you know what degree of pain the patient is having? Remember that different stressors contribute to pain and some people are more sensitive. We need to be proactive and not reactive. We need to get hold of the doctor and ask for more pain medication, or increased frequency, increased dosage, pain cocktails or different opiates. If you are not sure what to ask for, because pain control is a complex issue, get a resource book on pain control and give the doctor suggestions, especially if they are newly qualified. You are the person by the bedside, you are the patient's advocate. Call the doctor to get changes made, whatever the time of day or night. I don't care if you are concerned about the doctor's response at three in the morning. You and the doctor are not the patient lying in the bed experiencing the pain. Pain allowed to get out of control can run away with the patient, and the minutes can seem like hours. It then takes longer to get pain free again. Pain also has a damaging effect on sleep, appetite, mental outlook, stress levels and probably immune response. If the doctor isn't happy when you disturb him or her, remember he is not the one in pain and guess what? Next time he gets a patient who is terminal in his care, he'll remember to prescribe ample coverage for pain because he will **not** want to be woken again at three in the morning!

Nurses are the most appropriate people to help with the dying process in the hospital setting. They spend more time with the patient than anyone else and they are there during the long nights when the patient's fears are increased or more apparent because daytime noise and distractions are not there. Be prepared to listen, not to speak necessarily, but to be a mirror for the patient to express their fears. Be willing not to know the 'right' thing to say, to not always know the answers. Be present in the moment, 100% present in mind, heart and body, even if it is just for a few minutes. It is alright to feel vulnerable; it does not mean that you are weak or unprofessional if you feel tearful. You are a human being observing the frailty of life and you care. God or Higher Spirit can speak through you. We may not think we will know what to say or say it right, but if we trust that what we are going to say is for the patients benefit and higher good then it will be perfect. If we speak with love in our hearts, then what we say will be perfect in the moment, for that patient. It may not be the thing to say to another patient. You may need different words or timing for others, for we are all different, uniquely special. Think love and then speak.

Intimacy = Into me, see. See where I am at. See where I hurt. Be there and listen to me.

The patient–nurse relationship is unique and very privileged. We are privileged to be in the role of comforter, healer into death, like a midwife is a carer into life.

During the phase of dying, which can take hours, days, even weeks, ask open-ended questions. Ask if the patient has seen anything unusual or different. Have they had any out of body experiences? If you ask open-ended questions of people who have had a near-death experience (NDE), they will start to tell you their experiences. They tend not want to initiate the conversation because they are afraid that you will think they are 'losing it' or hallucinating. Initiating the subject involves risk of being laughed at or ridiculed and a NDE is usually too precious to the person for them to risk telling a relative, stranger or even close family.

I would like to see the aim for dying be that of making death as beautiful and meaningful as we can for each person, where there is time to attend to the details. A 'good' death is a gift, an acceptance, surrender and peaceful passing. We are all going to die; it's just a matter of when, where and how. So let us try to get it as right as possible for each individual, just as we would a birth or wedding.

Surrender can be seen as a weakness, a loss, a negative energy, a victim role. Yet I would implore you, the patient, to look at the strength of this word, the emotion, the energy. Surrender is to accept the situation you are in and be in control by getting your affairs in order. Surrender can be having faith that you are supported by a knowing guidance and that you entrust yourself to that guidance. Surrender is the hardest thing to do when you are scared. The act of surrendering is an act of courage, not weakness at all. In the middle of things, sometimes just saying, 'I let go and let God, or my higher wisdom, assist me' will be as if a light went on and you are more peaceful about your circumstances. Celebrate your willingness to surrender, for it is a time when you are close to your connection with Spirit and your God.

Currently, there are differing thoughts about euthanasia throughout the world. Some countries and states are organised and allow patients to choose their date of dying. Other countries fling their hands up in horror and refuse to allow this. As long as the patient is the one who has had enough and wants to die, is terminal and is not being over-pressured to do this; I personally think it is kinder. We put our pets down to help them and stop their suffering. Why would we not be given that same option? Please remember that you have to be of 'sound mind' to sign papers allowing this. So in the case of dementia please think ahead. Usually two doctors have to agree and sign the forms.

For those of us in the healthcare industry, we need to support the death and dying process by paying it full attention. We should study as much as we can so we can support our patients in their final days. By learning, we can help our patients, talking with them, being willing to take the time to talk, laugh, cry with them and show that we care. We need to make sure that our patients are as fully prepared and supported as much as possible for their journey. I have seen 'poor' deaths because of ignorance, fear and rigidity. The act of death itself is usually peaceful and a release, but the dying process can sometimes be difficult unless we properly prepare if we can. As I have already said, palliative care and hospice staff are great at this but approximately 50% of us will die in a regular hospital ward; so we should all be prepared.

Some Arrangements

Quality of life is of prime importance – why prolong life if death is inevitable? We need to be realistic about our goals. Life is about quality not quantity. Let's not hinder death in nursing homes, hospitals and hospices. Let us get to the stage of being able to know when it is time to let go, allowing the person go with pride, dignity and caring.

Sometimes relatives cannot bring themselves to give the authority to discontinue life support, such as ventilators. Even when the patient has been diagnosed as clinically dead, because relatives may have their own issues they are dealing with. They have not had time to say their goodbyes, maybe they feel guilty about a last conversation they had. So life gets unnecessarily prolonged because of uncertainties.

How much easier if you are given advanced warning that your time is coming to an end. The opportunity to be able to get your affairs straight, to say what you want to friends and family and for them to talk with you and find out what your wishes are.

Many of us are more likely to survive car crashes than die because of modern day medical treatments, both by paramedics at the accident scene and in hospital. However, we may be left in a coma or vegetative state. Especially young people who may drink and drive recklessly; so it is a good idea at any age to have a legal document stating how you wish to be treated in the event of being in a permanent vegetative state, or if you are dying soon. Better that you decide rather than leaving it up to others, relatives, doctors, even the court system. These documents are called 'Living Wills' or 'Advanced Directives' and should be written and reviewed periodically, specifying what you, the patient, want to have happen to you. Do you want antibiotics or heroic measures taken or do you want nothing done to prolong life? In which cases 'Do Not Resuscitate' (DNR) orders will be written. It is important to do this so that there are no unnecessary heroic measures suddenly taken in the last few hours of life. Sometimes a new nurse or doctor is on duty, unaware of your wishes, so having those wishes documented is essential so there are no questions. This also can sometimes happen because a relative suddenly appears on the scene and insists on everything being done.

If the patient's wishes are clearly defined, written down, signed, dated and witnessed, the medical professionals are less vulnerable to litigation and can have a freer hand to assist the patient with their wishes. Otherwise, there can be confusion and if a relative starts throwing their weight around, it makes the medical personnel nervous that there will be a legal problem. They will be less inclined to follow a verbal instruction if another person challenges it.

For example, if Joe's second wife/partner says, 'Joe wanted such and such', and then Joe's son by his first marriage (who happens to be a lawyer) arrives and says, 'Oh no, Dad would not want this to be done, and if you go ahead and do that, then I will sue you', then this just causes distress to all concerned.

So Joe is unconscious, unable to speak, and this battle starts up between the relatives. The doctors get anxious, there is no legal paperwork, questions have now arisen as to what Joe really wanted, and so they go the path of least resistance and start heroic measures because someone insists.

You can't blame the doctors, they are just human and don't want to lose their licenses, and their jobs. So Joe ends up on a ventilator and on antibiotics trying to fix a problem infection when he is dying from terminal cancer. This does happen; I have seen it happen several times.

There is no point in saying to yourself 'Well that's morbid and I don't want to discuss that or think about it'. That is like being an ostrich with its head in the sand or standing at the departure gate and not having a boarding pass! Realise that planning and foresight will make it easier on your relatives, friends, executors and medical personnel and will be of benefit to you also. Write down your wishes, put your signature on it, date it and have two independent witnesses sign and date it also. Ideally do it legally with the correct forms, ahead of the time, to cover all the bases.

Your Will

Now what is going to happen to all your worldly goods and chattels? Do you know that currently, only approximately 40%–50% of people have a written legal Will? Some people are too lazy, some think it is morbid, and some think that by writing a will their death will come sooner! Many people think they have nothing to give away, but when you start to add it together, it can be surprising what you do have. Even writing down which pictures, ornaments, jewellery you want to gift and to whom will help. Even little mementos can mean a lot to the recipients. The headache of not writing a will for families is just not worth it. It takes time to get monies released and affairs sorted out even when there is a clearly written, straightforward will. Not having a Will written causes all sorts of nightmare situations for families and loved ones left behind. Families can end up in huge rifts, not speaking for years over a 'problem'. It would be nice to think that everything will be rosy and communications clear; but old animosities arise and bitterness can surface after a person dies. Not having a will causes all sorts of problems. 'Aunt Bertha promised me the piano'. 'No, she promised it to me...', and so on.

When there is no will, your affairs go into probate and it can take years before your monies get released to the people you want it to go to, and it may go to the 'wrong' people because it is government lawyers who decide who gets what. This costs extra money and delays. Without a will, you may find that your piano went to the very last person you wanted it to go to. And there you will be, in Spirit, listening to your piano being played by someone you didn't like! And all you had to do was draw up a will. That is not being morbid; it is being wise and practical and it won't make you die sooner!

I recommend that you draw up a will as soon as you can. I wrote my first will when I was 26, because I was about to go travelling. I review it every few years and especially after someone who was to be a beneficiary dies.

In some countries, you can do a 'Do It Yourself Will'. You can either write it yourself or get a pre-printed form. Check what is legal in your specific country. In the United Kingdom, there is a difference because in England you can write your own Will, but in Scotland you have to have one done by a Solicitor. Usually you must have a will signed and dated by you and two witnesses to make it legal. When my uncle died he had a legal Will ready but in his last week he wrote a page of changes, an 'addendum'. He signed it but had not had it witnessed. My cousin and I as executors chose to follow his wishes as stated in the handwritten note, even though it was 'not legal'.

Donation of Your Organs and Body

Once you are clinically dead, you can still give the gift of life to others. With the wonders of medical transplants, there are many parts of you that can be recycled! Your eyes, heart, lungs, kidneys, liver and other organs can be transferred within a few hours after your death to others who need them. You can help someone to see again, or give them a healthy heart; you can give a real gift to another. However, this is something that is a very personal decision and should be discussed with your loved ones ahead of time and notification given to your doctor that you are willing to donate one or many of your organs. You can specify which organs if you like or you can donate your body to medical research. There are donor cards available that you can sign and carry with you in your wallet or purse, so that if you are suddenly taken to hospital the card is right there.

Some doctors are good at asking relatives right after death whether they would consider letting your organs be used; but many medical personnel are diffident at approaching newly bereft people and asking them to make that decision. So it is much easier to let your relatives know ahead of time what your wishes are, and by signing the donor card you are ensuring your wishes are met. In some countries, there is an assumption by law that your organs can be used unless you make it known in writing that you do not want that to happen. Many people currently die while waiting for an organ to become available. Please think seriously about giving someone a gift of a new organ and a new lease on their life.

Many medical schools are grateful for bodies for medical students to study, or for research.

The Personal Stuff

Most importantly let the people that you care about know that you care. If you love them, tell them so. Thank them for being part of your life, for having made a difference to your life. Give them space to let them speak about their love and care for you too. Don't wait until it is too late and be left with regrets for not having talked about how you feel.

I think this is true in any part of life, living or dying. I remember during 9/11, the phone calls made were about the loving and caring, and importance of people to the victims. That was what they really wanted to say when they thought they were about to die…not the stock market, or business.

If you are able to make amends, do so; say sorry to people you have done wrong to or hurt. You can even write a letter to ones who have died before you. Letter writing is amazingly cathartic. You can release a lot of inner bitterness and anger that you may have by writing it down. Then you can burn it, tear it up and throw it away or if they are still alive, send it to the person. Phone calls might be better but only if that feels right to you. I did this once to an ex-boyfriend who I had left abruptly and unkindly. It was my first relationship and I did not know any better. So I phoned him 20 years later and apologised. He was very surprised but it made me feel better as I had always felt guilty about how I had handled things. Try to mend the broken fence, figuratively. Let people know you are sorry for what you did, and you will be amazed at how much better you will feel. Try not to go to sleep on an argument or harsh words. My best friend died overnight and it would have been dreadful if we were arguing when he died.

Goodbye for Now – Clinical Events at Time of Death

I proceeded into nursing and saw people struggle and be fearful of death. Then they would die and in the instant of death, they would become peaceful, a look of peace would come across their faces, a serenity that was unexplainable.

I also observed the timing of death, the ones who would wait until they had seen a certain person, or the ones who would die just after or before the relatives got to their bedside.

My mother, after both her mother and husband had died with her not beside them kept saying that she wished that she had been there to hold their hand, that she would have liked to have been with them when it happened. I tried to reassure her that some spirits find it easier to leave when there is not a close family member there. This is because sometimes the relative doesn't want them to die and their energy keeps the spirit from leaving while they are in the room.

I practice Spiritual Healing, some call it Therapeutic Touch or Laying on of Hands, or Reiki. This is a touch therapy that helps calm people, that can lower blood pressure, improve sleep, reduce pain perception and aims to promote healing.

When I first started doing it on patients who were near to death, I would find that they would often die very shortly after I had been in their room. Initially, I was upset and thought that maybe, somehow I was harming them and causing them to die early. Was I somehow killing them off when I wasn't even touching them?

It took me a while to realise that actually people who are about to die need more energy, because the act of transition requires energy, and very often a dying person doesn't have enough energy to leave the physical body. Sometimes they are too weak physically to do this and they need to gather energy to assist them.

They always have the free will to decide if they are going to leave in this moment or the next, but they sometimes need a helping hand in the way of energy. They also sometimes need 'permission' to leave so when I do a healing session with a dying patient I always ask for healing of their body, mind and spirit, and tell them that they are free to move on if they feel ready to do so. I do this silently or verbally depending on the circumstances.

Loved ones and family tend to not want their loved one to leave. They are not ready to part with them. Things haven't been said, or have been, but maybe resolutions haven't occurred. Fear of abandonment, loss, unfinished business – there are many reasons why people are not ready to release their loved one and they hold onto the person physically, mentally and emotionally. They can hold on unconsciously and prevent the soul's departure or rebirth into the spiritual realm.

Other scenarios are people waiting to die who need to say something or complete unfinished affairs with a relative or friend, and they wait until that person can arrive and then the spirit leaves.

Others just seem to set a time when they are going. They will say, 'I will die on Friday' and they do. They close their eyes and are gone at their assigned time!

I had a young patient with cystic fibrosis, aged 27 years, who I had been caring for. I knew she wasn't doing well and her husband was with her most of the time. I came on duty and went into her room and she told me that she was about to die and that she had been waiting for me. She died within an hour of my coming to see her and her passing was very peaceful, leaving her distraught husband and myself crying at the end of her bed.

I had another patient, 25 years old, who just knew he was going to die after an operation. He wrote his 'final letters' the night before surgery, and despite the minimal surgical risk, and we nurses teasing him and trying to reassure him that he was going to be fine, he did indeed die within 24 hours of his surgery. In fact, he never regained consciousness from his surgery.

As I have said before, there is a common theme that I have noted in all the deaths that I have seen, where I have taken care of patients in the hospital. No matter if the events leading up to the moment of death are painful, fearful or peaceful and calm, there is a definite peaceful energy in the moment of death. There is a visible difference in their facial appearance. A look of serenity, peace and tranquillity is usually seen on the face of the person, a glow or aura of calm. There is a definite sense that the personality, the being, the energy that made up the person has gone and that what is left is simply the body case, the shell. It always feels that the person is gone, and only the body remains. I liken it to an empty suitcase; the contents have gone.

Clinically, the person is examined by a physician who checks the person's reflexes and listens for heart and breath sounds. On noting no heart or breath sounds for a few minutes, the physician proclaims that the patient is dead and notes the time of death. The body is then taken care of, depending on hospital protocol and also depending on the person's religion. The body is washed, wrapped in a shroud and removed to the hospital morgue. There may be an autopsy if cause of death is questionable. Then the body is collected by an undertaker or mortician and removed to the funeral home where it is prepared for the wake, showing and funeral.

Aim for a 'good death' at whatever age you are.

Chapter 9

Dealing with Life Afterwards

For those of us who are left behind after our loved one has died and gone before…

How do we cope and get on with the rest of our lives? Firstly, please do not feel guilty if you laugh. It is a form of release of tension and stress. Also, it is a way of remembering your loved one. You laughed together when they were with you, so why not laugh now and remember the funny times? Your loved one does not want you to be overly serious. Remember that in many countries, death is seen as a celebration that your loved one has gone to their God.

The first couple of weeks after death is a busy time. Registering the death, contacting relatives, organising the undertaker or funeral director, arranging for the church service, hymns, prayers, after-service wake or party. Notifying friends, businesses, closing bank accounts, a flurry of activity.

If you are able to, take the time to go and see the body of your loved one; whether it is at the mortuary, undertakers or at home. You can touch and talk to the body and realise that the essence, the person you know is not there. It is just a body, like an envelope.

This will be an individual choice but it is a way of saying goodbye and making it real; especially if you were not there with the person when they died.

I came home from America after my father died and it seemed right to go and see him visibly, rather than just see a coffin that his body was in. I am glad I did as it gave me a chance for a more personal, real goodbye.

You may be exhausted after taking care of someone who has been very sick for a long time. Rest and be gentle with yourself. It is almost like being a convalescent. Don't expect too much of yourself. You may find you get irritable, tired, weepy when you least expect it. Go easy on yourself, call friends and ask for help. People like the opportunity to help but don't want to intrude or interfere.

Do not 'should' on yourself. Wherever possible, take it gently and slowly.

Cry if you want to, crying releases tension and is simply energy-in-motion (E-motion.) Let it come up and out. You will get over the acuteness more easily if you let grief come up as and when it needs to.

We in the Western world tend to do too much 'stiff upper lip' behaviour. The Eastern world is much better at emoting, crying openly and wailing and I think it eases the pain and grief, aiding the path to recovery.

Some religions suggest a year of official mourning. They feel it takes that time to allow for grieving. Some religions bury the body within 24 hours, some not for 72 hours.

There are people who wear black armbands or black dress for months, years or life.

Usually, there is an element of shock; even if it has been a long illness. When the event actually occurs, there is a sense of 'it can't be happening'. Even if death is a grateful release, there is still sadness, a sense of loss, grief.

Timing of Grief

When does grief come to the surface?

Minutes after receiving the news, days, months or years later. It can be a constant feeling or intermittent. It can arise over something obvious and over nothing at all.

Talk about it with counsellors, friends or not, keeping it to yourself. Do whatever feels right for you. Just allow yourself to be as you are and let it take time.

Grief is an emotion that comes out in all sorts of ways, or not at all. It can be all consuming, incapacitating and/or soft and gentle, a little bit at a time.

Anger, stiff upper lip, nightmares, sorrow, laughter; any and all of these emotions are appropriate. I personally did not cry over my father initially but 'saw' him by his bonfire area, several weeks later and promptly burst into tears. One very close friend who died unexpectedly, I kept crying about and also got very cross with him. The reason for this was I had planned on seeing him again and his dying was 'not part of the plan'!

Yet another close friend died suddenly and I had known her for 46 years and we were very close; yet two years later I still cannot cry. So grief comes differently for each occasion and person. It is all alright.

Keepsakes

Keep clothes, photos, objects, whatever feels right to you. Smells on clothing are a great reminder and memory aid; and so is music. I keep a shirt and tie of a friend of mine and when I feel lonely and in need, I touch them, hold them. Somehow, it makes him feel closer to me on a physical level, and brings me peace.

Sorting Out the Belongings

Maybe you have to sell a home, emptying and moving the contents. Again, if you can, TAKE TIME. Time gives you perspective; it lets you come out of the shock of bereavement, so you can think more clearly. Better to hold on to this stuff than get rid of it too soon.

Do Not Argue over the Will

The will is the dead person's decision over how they want to have their money and possessions shared out to ones they love, or don't! There are also legal guidelines which need to be followed. However, if there are grievances and different hurts and objections, voice them if you must, but honour the dead person's wishes to the best of your ability. Get out of the mentality of greed, poor me, victim role; embrace whatever gifts you have been given, be grateful and move on. You don't want Aunt Bertha coming to meet you at the Pearly Gates and telling you off for being selfish and greedy, do you?

Likewise, if you have been the luckiest recipient and you know that there have been people left out, or not fairly done by; see if you can affect some change in the will, for their benefit also. Let it be a win/win situation. Be magnanimous and let some of your blessings go to others who have been less blessed. Do what feels right, remembering the dead person's wishes and how you would like to be treated.

Chiefly, please do not argue with your siblings. Your relationship with your siblings and family members are much more important than any article or money. The things or money may seem important at the time, especially when emotions are running high, but you cannot replace family and relationships. Remember that you may well meet up again with the deceased one who will give you more grief if you argue over money and things, at the expense of love and cherishment.

Some untold misery can come from the heat of the moment. I know of at least two families in my area where there are three siblings who no longer talk with each other because of disagreements over property distribution.

If one person is being overly bossy or controlling in order 'to help'. 'To get the job done so things can get back to normal as quickly as possible'. Try to remember that it is their way of trying to cope with their feelings and emotions.

Life Is Too Short to Argue

Yes you will probably have words and emotions, but do not let the sun go down on an argument. It is simply not worth it.

Advice for Friends of the Bereaved

Bereavement can be a lonely place as people don't know what to say, for fear of saying the 'wrong thing' and upsetting the bereaved person. After the funeral, in the weeks and months ahead, the bereaved can feel very abandoned and alone. Not just because of their loss, but also because friends avoid them, tiptoe around them, avert their eyes, cross the street to 'not interfere', or because they 'don't know what to say'. Just because you may not know what to say, or are afraid of saying the wrong thing or upsetting the grieving person, do it anyway.

'I don't know what to say', 'I don't want to intrude'. 'She seems to be handling it so well, I might mess up and say something to upset her'.

This is all the self-talk we give ourselves to avoid feeling awkward talking to the recently bereaved, for fear of upsetting them.

Please talk to your friend or neighbour. Reach out and do it; think of them, not you. It is not about how you will feel; it is about the bereaved person and helping them in their hour of need.

It is better to do something than nothing. Sharing some warmth and intimacy is a true gift to your friend. A friendly gesture, a handshake, a hug, 'I'm so sorry'; it just opens up the humanness, the connection.

If a child was hurting, you would try to console them; we adults are no different. We are children in grown-up bodies. So what if you both burst into tears; what a lovely way of showing you care.

Invite them for dinner if you used to entertain the person as part of a couple. Similar to a separated or divorced couple many people, especially women, notice that they are no longer invited to occasions like dinner parties as people don't know what to do with them as a 'singleton'. Remember they are a person like you and they are hurting, so reach out and take extra care of them if you feel able.

Put yourself in their shoes and go give them a non-verbal hug, a squeeze of the hand, show them you hurt for them. Support them as best you can. Much better to say to yourself, 'I did what I could' than to say 'I should have, and did not'. So much better to do something, rather than nothing.

After the funeral, there can be a pause of a month or two. During this time you notify the various authorities and banks, and papers arrive with statements from various banks and financial investments.

You have to gather all this information and submit it to government officials for assessment. The value of the deceased person's property is evaluated and you may have to pay inheritance tax costs. Often people ask their solicitor or attorney to sort this out for them, which naturally you pay for. However, you usually are the one that gathers the information and then submits it to the lawyer who collates it all and sends to the government department. I found that in my mother's case, I did the paperwork myself. In Scotland, I was given paperwork from the government to assist me in filing the papers. If I had a question I could call them up and they would help me with the details. Consequently, it took me a few days to fill out the necessary details. It saved me quite a lot of money doing the paperwork myself.

If the choice has been cremation, you will eventually be given the ashes in a container or urn. My friend wanted to have his ashes scattered over a bridge. As I did this, I felt his presence beside me and a flock of pelicans flew under the bridge in a 'missing man formation', with the straggler flying to join the others about a minute later. I really felt that was all part of the ceremony. Several of my relations ashes are scattered around my large garden, so they are always with me!

When and only if you are ready, go and see a reputable medium or go to a Spiritualist Church. I would encourage you to go to a few services. You may receive a message at the first service you go to or you may not get one for a few services. You will get a feel for the type of service, the style of speaker and the quality of the connections. The quality is key; there are excellent mediums and some not so gifted. Remember the promise of the gifts from the Holy Spirit; speaking and healing.

Good detailed connection with spirit takes practice and as in all walks of life, there are good mediums and some not quite so good.

Just like various Pastors, Rabbis, Preachers, Imams and Priests, some are riveting and some are less so. If you are lucky enough to get a good connection with your loved ones via a medium, you will know beyond a shadow of doubt. You will feel it to be true and know it to be true that your loved ones do live on at a different vibrational energy. That there is no death of who you truly are. That life is continuous, just in a different form.

A good communication should give you proof of the spirit connecting with you. A significant meaningful message that makes sense to you and bring you peace, contentment and reassurance that your loved one does indeed live on; it is just that you can no longer see them physically.

The service in a Spiritualist Church normally consists of prayers, hymns and spoken inspiration. The only difference is there will be a speaker/medium who is able to 'sense' either with sight, sense or hearing, the presence of spirit. Usually a spirit presence is trying to bring a message of comfort and hope to someone in the audience. There is a sequence or pattern for this to occur:

The medium identifies the relevant person in the audience and asks permission to work with them. Some kind of proof from the spirit world that the spirit energy coming through is connected to the audience member, usually by relating a memory, event, that makes sense to the person. On confirmation the medium asks permission to continue the contact. They may give more information. Finally, the message that the spirit wants to say is brought through.

When a good connection is made, the energy in the room is electric, emotional and there is no doubt that there is truth there. The message is clear and makes an impact.

The recipient is truly touched on an emotional level by the words spoken and usually there is much healing and peace and reassurance that their loved one lives on and is still 'nearby'. I believe this can ease the degree of grief being experienced.

You could say that it is a hoax, all made up, but just go to a good medium, an intermediary for Spirit and see how moving, real and true the experience is and then doubt; if you choose to.

Other religions tend to condemn the Spiritualist movement, claiming it to be 'devil work'. Yet the Spiritualist Movement is actually trying to prove and give evidence of what all other religions are talking about. Everlasting life, life after death! They talk about it in their services, yet Spiritualists are actually trying to do more than that; they make contact in order to give proof. Why does this threaten the 'regular' religions?

However, recently, Spiritualism is becoming much more mainstream and during this pandemic, memberships of online churches are increasing rapidly as people seek reassurance. I would suggest that you wait at least six months before you go to see a medium, because you need time to adjust to the loss.

Do not become over-dependent on seeing a medium often. You need to be able to move forward. Grieving and seeking reassurance is normal, but you still have your own life to lead. So do not get stuck in over-grieving at the expense of living your life. Know that you will reconnect in the future.

Your partner, parent, child or friend who has gone ahead of you would want you to continue to live your life fully. Remember them, and smile that you knew and loved them and still can.

Chapter 10

'Avoiding the Void' No Longer

Most of us spend our lives avoiding the 'Void', that feeling of emptiness. This is often felt in our stomach and gut area, the empty space where we wonder who we are and why we are here.

We numb out this empty feeling with food, drink, smoking, drugs overwork, cars, things and money. We try to get control with power, try to satisfy our need, our yearning for that illusive something; that fix. We don't know why we have this need, this empty hollow feeling. Despite everything, we have and do, all our successes, achievements, all that we attain, the Void is still there.

'If only… If I got… I'd be happy'.

The next car, next girlfriend, the next guru, the next promotion is the thing that will ease or cease the void! And it might, but just for a short time. However, it is always just out there in front of us, always elusive and out of reach. We try to avoid feeling this void, and fill it up with anything that helps us go numb so that we do not feel the emptiness.

It makes us search and stretch and be restless, and we don't know why.

Avoiding the void by being busy doing, getting, obtaining, keeping busy no matter what! Another sport, trophy, award, degree. A new recipe, new restaurant, the next film. Sexual orgasm, winning the jackpot, getting the new shiny car makes us happy for a while... but then the feeling of lack, emptiness, 'What's it all about?' returns.

I feel mine in my stomach and so I overeat to fill this hole, this Void, to fill up to saturation level, but it is never enough. I fill up and feel full, numb, comforted for a while and then the cycle starts again. The craving, the yearning, the ever searching need to fill the ever-empty hole from without. We keep trying to fill this void that we are only half conscious of. It eludes us and we are so busy eluding it; avoiding the void.

It has taken me many years and much pain emotionally to discover that the answer is never from outside ourselves.

I believe that the way to fill the void is by going within. We tend to search outside ourselves for the satisfaction that we should learn how to seek inside.

The hole we are trying to avoid is our lack of connection with our spiritual home, our 'ah' place within.

The secret is to search within. Be where you are exactly now. Be fully aware of where you are now.

Look around and be grateful for all you have. The shirt on your back, health, wealth, a roof over your head, friends, job, whatever it is. Be thankful that you have life and breathe and the chance of filling the Void, now that you have awareness; as awareness is 90% of getting it. The rest is just starting to do it.

Stop avoiding the void and start to fill it with your own inner connectedness with spirit.

Once the Void is acknowledged and heard, it will be less needy. Start to feel it and explore it. What is it for you? What do you search for or hope for with your new job, new car? Is it a warm fuzzy feeling, a 'superior than you' feeling, a whole feeling, a peaceful feeling. What?

And where do you feel it in your body when you feel the void. It will be different for all of us. What turns someone on may well turn someone else off. Essentially, we are the same with our wants and desires; there is nothing wrong with these. They get us out of bed in the morning and get us out there into the world to live our lives.

But we could make it so much easier on ourselves. How? By listening to your void, ignoring it no longer. Start to enjoy getting to know it and learn how to fill the empty hole up.

Initially, it will feel uncomfortable not knowing it, of having avoided it all these years. Once familiar with your void, it will give you valuable feedback for your future needs.

All these years you have asked yourself 'Is this all that there is?' And looked out there, outside yourself to try and find satisfaction. You have found a goal, made a plan of how to achieve it and accomplished it. There is nothing wrong with that. Goals and aims are very important. However, alongside, you need to be in touch with your void and check out how you truly feel inside now, and now,... as days, weeks and months go by.

Your feelings and desires may change, and by checking in, you will be on top of the void's (your) needs. Remember that your needs may well be different from your friends.

Getting to Know Your Void

Stop living in the past and future... 'back packing' and 'future tripping'.

Be conscious of the present, the now. What you are doing right now with your life?

Are you seeing the people you are walking past? Are you realising that they are souls and spirits just like you, trying to do their best in their world with all their limitations and history and baggage?

Mindfulness is being aware. Mindfulness meditation is being aware in the moment as you are doing things. Stop being on 'auto pilot,' and start to truly drive yourself. This life of yours is your trip, your journey; no one else's. Are you driving it as you would like?

Be aware of your breath as you walk from A to B, be concious; acknowledge the next person you pass by with a look and smile.

You'll be amazed how often you get smiled at, once you start smiling, genuinely, from the inside. It is not just the smile the people see; it is the energy you are radiating as you do it that they pick up on. So smiling while you say to yourself "I hate this guy" will probably not get you a smile in return! You have to feel it, but it is OK to 'act as if' until you can genuinely do it. It is said that it takes 3-4 weeks to make something a habit. Let it be a game and you will be surprised how quickly it just becomes part of who you are. For we all truly want to be liked and want to help others, given the chance. We have sometimes forgotten how due to our battles along the way.

Keep bringing yourself back into the now. Be present for the present. Most of us are driving along thinking of jobs, kids, shopping. Suddenly, we realise we have got where we were going without really knowing how we got there!

Be consciously present, in as much of your life as you can be, moment to moment.

Check in with your void, your feeling register. Give your void a name if you wish.

It will give you all sorts of feedback and awareness that you have never had before.

It can be your companion, guide, friend if you give it the chance.

We are so used to looking 'out there' for the experts to show us how to live our life – to our parents, teachers, coaches, gurus, bosses, partners etc.

How you live your life for them may be fine for them. But you are the one inhabiting your body and you are the one who truly knows your 'ah ha' times and what you need to do about it. Let your 'ah ha' be your chief guide. Have other helpers, listen to others' feedback, but always go back inside to your higher self, your inner wisdom and see what IT is saying and telling you. It never shouts. It never calls you bad names. It is always a quiet inner peaceful warm loving voice, sense or feeling. Discount any internal voice that is loud, angry, negative or critical of you. That is possibly an old voice or habit you are recalling. Always be kind to yourself. Treat yourself as you would treat a dear friend.

How to get most familiar with your void takes time. Sit daily for at least 15 minutes with no distractions. Ideally do it in a quiet place, alone, at a time of day that suits you. I find early-morning works best for me as I am too tired by the end of the day. Take a few deep breaths and bring your awareness into your central part, at heart or stomach area. Feel your empty spot, your own personal void and let it know that you are no longer going to ignore and avoid it by being busy, too numb or too....

Meditation is a great way to get in touch with yourself and your inner self. You can develop this to feel in tune with the Infinite; your Higher Self, Spirit, God; whatever you want to call it. It is like tuning into a radio wave. To hear a good tune clearly requires fine-tuning. You have to dial in to the right waveband and that takes a little practice.

Doing it daily makes it easier and quicker to tune in; and the experience is different every time.

You will find that as you do it you will start to begin to fill that void, that empty hole bit by bit, like grains of sand filling a well. It will not happen overnight, but then nothing worth doing is done overnight. It takes 6 years to become a doctor, 12 years to get through school, 9 months to mature a baby.

It takes 3 weeks to start a habit so give yourself at least a month to try.

If you like it, keep going. If you don't, then stop.

What have you got to loose? Nothing; you actually have everything to gain.

Believe me I have spent 40 years avoiding my void with travel, jobs, relationships, food, drink, sports, always keeping busy. Great when you get the achievements, but usually only momentary satisfaction and then the void would start to growl again and the search starts up again.

I spent years dabbling occasionally with meditating, 'going within'. I would stop practicing at every chance; even though on some level I knew it was good for me and that I felt better when I did do it. But I think I was scared of the changes it might bring about in me and the 'what if…?'

What if I could not handle these ideas, changes? What if it would bring about change, uncertainty and more restlessness into my life? Well I was already restless, wanting change on some level, often searching for something, but not sure what.

By starting to meditate, giving myself the space of fifteen minutes and stopping sooner if it was too long for that day; bit by bit I found I wanted more. The 'Lay in bed, do not disturb' person was suddenly setting the alarm a little earlier so I could meditate. Why?

Because it helped me feel more content, centred and ready for the day. It made me feel that I could cope more easily with life.

It made me feel more connected to myself. Meditation may not be right for someone else but they do not have my void, my story, my needs, my experiences and my tastes. So going out there to a guru or teacher to tell you what to do can be helpful but not as effective as going within to learn about your own inner tuition; intuitiveness.

Most good gurus, guides and teachers will tell you they can give you guidelines, ideas, tools, but it is within you. That you have **your** inner knowledge and no one else can do it for you. You are the one sitting here in this body, your being. So go inside and get to know your own void. Stop avoiding your void and it will become your best friend, your inner teacher, your guide, your buddy, your reference point.

Some of us go to church, temple, synagogue and mosque; partly because our parents taught us to, or our schools and we had religious education. People keep going because it fills a hole, they like the habit or ritual, the familiarity gives them comfort. Religious gatherings give some people a certain something, a certainty in this uncertain life.

Actually, that certainty is also very much within us. We can learn to go inside and get warm and comfy inside and get our feedback from our own knowing, our own guidance, our own connection with ourselves, spirit, god, higher consciousness, wisdom; whatever you want to call it.

You have been trying not to listen to it by all your doing, keeping busy. Now, instead of doing, be a being and just be for a short while daily. See what profound changes can occur, what inner riches you have.

Sit for the presence and receive the present of knowing yourself, your inner wisdom and connection. I think you will find much contentment from the experience.

The truth is that the emptiness, the hollow feeling in our core can really only be filled by love, love of self, not selfish love but realisation that we are spirit. We are spirit, not in spirit land but in this physical world and it is not easy, and we miss our 'home'.

We all want to find our home, which is actually inside us. Getting in touch with our 'ah ha' centre is key to reducing this sense of emptiness; than no amount of money, power, things, people, holidays will be able to do.

No one, no person can do it for us. Only by us going inside can we achieve a sense of inner peace, harmony and a fullness or inner contentment. Finding inner peace by meditating and being loving and gentle and kind to yourself will help you find it.

Once you become familiar with that feeling, that sense of not being alone in this world but a feeling of inner fullness, life will feel less of a struggle.

That is why people who have had a near-death experience feel that they don't want to return to their bodies. They get a sense of completeness, contentment and they don't want to return to the struggle of being alone in their physical body, trying to cope with living.

Meditation is a form of release and escapism. Why do you think monks, nuns and some meditators do it for hours a day, for years? Because it feels good, it is natural, it hurts no one and it helps you feel connected and filled. It gives you a perspective that allows you to cope more easily with the daily frustrations of life.

If we teach ourselves to start doing it and then teach our children how to do it, what a difference we will see in our world. It all starts with you; not the other guy. If you wait for the other guy, you will wait forever. There are schools that are now starting to teach very young children how to meditate as part of their lessons. Apparently they enjoy it, and what a great way to teach them about their own inner selves.

My Version of How to Meditate

Keep it simple. Give yourself initially 15–30 minutes at a time of day when you know that you can be least disturbed by wife, child, pet, phone, work etc. Late at night you may be too tired. Unplug the phone. Ritual is not necessary, but can help. Lighting a candle in a safe container, incense if you wish. Music can be an aid but can be distracting to the subtle points and ideas and creative thoughts that will pass through your mind.

Get comfortable, uncross arms and legs and have your back straight. I find that sitting up is best. In bed with legs slightly bent or straight. Use a chair or cushion on the floor. If you can get into fancy poses, or very bent knees, so be it, but being comfortable and warm is key.

Part your lips slightly. This helps the energies to move within you. Some say to touch the tip of the tongue on the roof of the mouth. I find that letting the tongue hang in the middle of the mouth, not touching the roof of the mouth is easier and stops the mental thinking from going on. It allows for a quicker quieting of the mind to occur. I also use that tongue position if I cannot sleep for thinking too much and find it very helpful.

Then just be, sitting not doing anything. You can take a few deep breathes and then breath normally and just be in your own space. Some breathe in for the count of 4, hold the breath for a count of 6 and then exhale over a count of 8 and repeat that 3 times for quicker centring/ settling down.

Thoughts will come into your head; this is normal. Let them pass through your mind, like a cloud crossing the sky. Do not attach your mind to the thought, just let it pass.

If one thought is very persistent, such as a shopping item, quickly write it down on a notepad beside you for following up later. Once written down you will be able to let it go. The focus is to slow down the thoughts more and more so the gap between the clouds (thoughts) is bigger and longer.

Be present for the present – you may see lights behind your eyes. You may see swirls of patterns; just go with it. You may get a sense of expansion, of inner warmth, lightness, a glow like sunlight coming behind your eyelids. You will, if you are like me, open your eyes to check if the sun has come out from behind a cloud. It may have; or it might be your own lightness of being making its presence felt. This helps you become aware that you are more than this physical body…so much more.

Set yourself a time for when you want to finish. You will find that you are drawn to ending at around that time. I recommend no more than half an hour for the first few months. If you find you wish to do more than that; then go for it.

Remember, it has its own level of healthy addictiveness. So make sure you are not meditating at the expense of getting your regular everyday stuff done!

Enjoy learning that you have a fullness within, that still small voice of information, reassurance. You may not hear an actual voice but you may hear yourself thinking thoughts that inspire you. A knowing or a thought that you wonder where it came from; an inspiration, idea, creative image that you have never had before.

Take a few minutes at the end of the session to write down any meaningful experiences or ideas you came up with. You can also ask specific questions before going into meditation and may get the answers there and then or perhaps through a friend's comment, an article that catches you eye, a book you come across shortly afterwards. Please make sure you are fully awake before you start the rest of your day;...a glass of water can help.

Being in the 'zone' is a modern day label for imagery and thinking yourself into a good functional state. It has been discovered that the brain has a 'plasticity'. So by visualising and thinking of some action, for example, running well; can make your body believe it is doing it. The power of positive thinking; 'being in the zone'.

The difference between that and meditating is there is brain visualisation and mental doing, versus reducing mental 'doing' and being brain still, which is not easy.

Both work well but the meditation and being in the 'ah' state is more for feeding your soul, your essence. Now if you did the meditation most days and then practiced being in the 'zone', you could well be unstoppable!

The chief reason for meditation I find is that it makes my day go better. I get less ruffled with the pressures of traffic, work, phone calls, other people's issues, I go more calmly through my day, worrying less about the extraneous issues. I achieve what I need to get done more effectively. I feel a warmth, an inner fullness and less tired. The stress factors are still around but they bother me less; I can shrug them off more easily. I am in more of a state of inner peace, yet functioning at a high level. I have less need to fill up at the end of the day with excess alcohol, food and purchases. I snap less at others and as I am less snappy, others around me are also more comfortable, less fractious and more at peace and in harmony. Less yelling, shouting, blame, attack goes on. There is less 'war' in my home and more peace.

You can search out there in the world;
then come home to find it within you.

Chapter 11

'Nirvana' Here and Now

And how do we get a bit of heaven on earth…Nirvana Now?

Start with you. Only you can make changes that will affect your world.

Make peace with yourself. Look inside you and realise you are only human, you make mistakes and you try your best. Love yourself and make peace with yourself first.

Forgive yourself of your imperfections. You are spirit trying to learn lessons in a physical body. Don't be so hard on yourself. It is alright to make mistakes; you can learn from them. Be kind to yourself as you would be with a dear friend.

Become aware of what makes you fearful. We have a choice to be fear-based or love-based. Being fear-based is limiting and expresses itself as anger, jealousy, worry and selfishness.

Love-based is expansive, loving, happy, content, with inner peace; trusting in the process of life and life's events.

Reduce the negative messages you give yourself. Some of these are unconscious.

It is just a habit that we have got in, to be fear-based, giving ourselves negative self-talk; focusing on negative gossipy media such as TV, radio and Internet chat rooms.

Stop watching so much news on TV. Reduce the amount of programmes you hear or see that are trashy or negative.

Limit the hate-driven video games that you and your children watch with their susceptible young minds. Where does reality and 'fiction' or 'real-lifelike' images blur in your mind or in those young minds you are trying to educate?

Learn to promote the positive within your home and reduce the negative. Positive comments can have an impact and gain rich rewards.

Focus on the positive and peaceful loving part of you. Release the unconscious fear-based thoughts that can run you and ruin your inner peace and contentment. Start to live and come from a place of inner peace. By doing this, you will change how you feel daily and your world will appear different.

God, as you know Him, is a caring loving Good God, and is all around us and within us. If we make Him the centre of our universe, aim to do good and connect with our spiritual centre, we will be more peaceful, content and secure.

Once you make peace with yourself and learn how to create inner peace, then you will exude it. Not in a hippy style 'peace brother' way, but in the way you naturally are. Once you are able to be at peace with yourself, then you will radiate it outwards. You can't help but do this, as your essence will be of a loving, peaceful energy.

Then make peace with your partner, children, family and friends. Then neighbours and work colleagues. There will be some whom you cannot make peace with. Try to see the God within them, which can be hard to do at times. Forgive them anyway and move on. Good for you and shame on them that they were too fearful to be big enough to make peace. They are the sufferers, not you.

You can also ask forgiveness of those who have died; they do hear you.

You cannot change the world but you can change yourself and your perspective on life. Your change will have an effect on those nearest you. Your inner peacefulness will impact them and they will change because of it, and so the ripples go out like a pebble being thrown into a pond. The outward rings expand but the origin, the start of this effect is in the middle...You!

By you affecting a change in your own 'mini' world, you change your surroundings, your universe. Others will be impacted by you and so it spreads out. More ponds will merge together and become lakes, then rivers and seas and so change in the World occurs.

Where there is fear – sow love.

The Prayer of St Francis

Lord, make me an instrument of your peace.
Where there is hatred, let me sow love.
Where there is injury, pardon.
Where there is doubt, faith.
Where there is despair, hope.
Where there is darkness, light.
And where there is sadness, joy.
O Divine Master.
Grant that I may not so much seek.
To be consoled as to console.
To be understood as to understand.
For it is in giving that we receive.
It is in pardoning that we are pardoned.
And it is in dying that we are born to eternal life.

Where you see conflict, try making peace. Anywhere, down the street, on a bus, a plane, in your workplace.

Gossip hurts so only speak of people as if they were standing beside you, with respect.

Respect yourself so that you can respect others. Do a good day's work if you can. Stop sponging off someone else, or the 'system'.

Care for one other person each day. Smile at your next door neighbour, a passing stranger.

'A stranger is a friend you have not yet met'.

Tell your family and friends that you love them; if you do. There are many types of love, loving your cat, dog, garden, friend and lover. Don't put off letting someone know that you care about them.. Why wait for the funeral service to bring flowers, cards and say how much you loved them or thought of them. Tell them while you and they are alive, not dead!

Have enough money for your security, but don't be greedy. So many of our problems are based on greed, power and always wanting more. More money, power, status, land, country, oil etc.

Ask yourself 'When is enough, enough?'

Encourage your children to be the best they can be; but not at the expense of others. Don't be overcritical of them; they need gentle guidance. Encourage teamwork and the concept of all being winners. Aim for a win/win solution. Instead of an either/or; or having to win at someone else's expense.

I believe that I am a spiritual being and I am trying to live a spiritual life to the best of my ability. However, I do not consider myself a religious person because I feel religion can tend to be too limited and restrictive. There are many sects of various religions and each one is important to the people who attend that religion. The structure, ritual, ornamentation, companionship and support they offer is very important to a lot of people; they need that in their lives and they need it to help feel closer to God. My own concern with religion is that each religion believes, and some more than others, that their way is the *only* way to salvation. They believe that the rest of the religions are to be left behind and are less important than theirs. I believe we need to have the freedom to choose how we believe, to choose how we pray and let others have their freedom also.

To condemn or put down other religions is to put God down because all religions have a common theme. They worship a Higher Being, God, Allah, etc. The pattern of worship may be different but the core belief is the same. We all try to be better people, gain spiritual enlightenment and worship something bigger and better than ourselves. So no religion is the only way, or the right way, and none is better than another. God loves us all equally so why would we be treated so differently by Him? I believe it is not God that treats us differently.

I believe it is religious dogma that encourages us to treat others differently. God did not make religion. Man did, for his own reasons. We are all children of God, spiritual beings traveling on different paths trying to do the best we can until we get back HOME from where we all came.

So let us learn to respect all faiths, allowing each their freedom to walk the path they choose without condemning them or making them wrong because they choose to worship in a different way to how you were taught or choose to worship.

Let us learn to love each other, love our differences and learn from them, not fear them. Our differences can enrich us and broaden our outlook, increasing our understanding and appreciation for life. Be open minded about other religions. We are all trying to be better people; otherwise some of us would not be going to a religious service. We wish we were more God-like and better able to follow our religions and beliefs. God is magnanimous and is all loving, embracing and forgiving.

Religions are manmade and flawed with their desire for control, power, money and rule. The limitations and bigotry start not with God, but with the men who want to have the power and control. Did you know that in Bethlehem, three different religions manage the Church of the Nativity where Jesus supposedly was born? The shame is they apparently constantly fight each other, even with fists on occasion!

Getting to God and being more God-like is similar to God being at the top of a mountain. There are many paths up the mountain, they all start at the bottom, and work up to the top, where God is. Some paths are on the east face, some are on the north, south and west face of the mountain. They are all hard and climbed differently. One path is Christian and all the various denominations of Christianity. Other paths are Islam, Hindu, Buddhist, etc. However you get there – whether it is through the Torah and Passover or The Koran and Ramadan or The Bible and Easter – we are all the same.

It does not matter whether you are bending down on one knee, or both knees, or praying to the west or east, God does not care, as long as we focus some attention on Him. God loves us all. I would encourage you to explore different religions and take what you like and leave the rest.

Anyone who wants to make war is either power hungry or lusting after some form of it or living in fear. Wanting more money, power, control and wealth. Often this is the real reason for going to war, not the 'patriotic' reasons that are given. Even a 108-year-old veteran of World War I, 90 years after war said, 'It was wrong to go to war'. Remember the German victims and sufferers as well as the side that 'won'. No one wins, not really, and any victory is bitter sweet.

Reach out a hand of friendship rather than picking up arms. Decline to go to war –there is nothing wrong with doing that. Be a peace maker rather than a killer.

Why is it alright to take the life of a person in the name of war and kill in the name of God or your country; yet not alright to take the life of an unborn baby or to not euthanise a person dying of a painful fatal condition who is suffering and wants to be released. Why such mixed messages and values about precious human life? Why does life stop being precious in times of war?

If the political leaders who decide to go to war, actually physically had to go to war themselves; I bet there would be less speed to kill and more patience to negotiate.

Most wars are fought by young men who are asked to risk their lives 'for God and Country'. God does not want you to risk your life for Him by going to war. He does not need your dead body or your enemies' bodies to prove anything to Him. Your family and your enemies' families all want you not to have to go to war. They want you to be safe; not to die in vain for some politicians' gain, greed, hunger or self-righteousness.

Peace and non-violence are the real answer. Gandhi and Martin Luther King are our lighthouses for peace, to mention just two. War and God are not words that go together. Leaders of all religions have a lot to be answerable for, if they encourage any death of another human being.

Fighting others because they are climbing a different face of the mountain to God is crazy, and leaders of all religions should be ashamed of themselves if they partake in encouraging in any way this belief.

If you want to go and battle, and get rid of some of your 'man' raging hormones go and battle disease, poverty, hunger, ignorance and speak His name in Love and Peace. God's representatives, prophets Jesus, Allah, Buddha spoke of love and honouring our fellow man, never of war for any reason. God, Allah is Love, and needs no one to fight for Him. He is too big and loving to care about the petty squabbles of Man. He wants our love and our caring of others and our peace to reflect his values.

What if everyone refused to pick up arms and go to war? With no one doing it, war could not happen. Maybe we should all take a stand for Peace.

Fear can have many faces. Fear of the bully, fear of loss of face, loss of power, shame, anger or greed. All based on fear of not being or having enough. Going to war for your country is not always patriotic. The whole world is your country and all nations your countrymen. You are all children of God –'The Brotherhood and Sisterhood of Man'. If the politicians want to go to war, let them go to war. Make peace, like Mahatma Gandhi. War kills, and no one truly wins, as history can tell us. Peaceful non-violence will achieve so much more and help to protect our countries and planet earth.

Love is a much more powerful emotion that can change the world, how we see it and how we are in it. Love of our self, our partners, children, parents, neighbours, friends and community. Responsible love that becomes response-able. Able to respond, to help in times of difficulty, empowering others to help themselves.

Look at the world around your doorstep. How can you make a difference today? Clean up some graffiti, plant a seed or pull a weed. Help a friend and neighbour, smile at a stranger. Every little bit helps us as people, no matter what our skin colour is.

It takes fewer muscles to smile than frown and a smile will give you a lift, a frown will bring you down as well as others!

In the bible are many references to the Voice of God, and Angels sending messages to His People. Spirit has historically always spoken to us through people. In modern times, there are people who 'channel'. Seers, psychics and mediums, people who can link in with and give messages from the 'other side'. We all get 'inspirations', (inner wisdom) ideas and can choose to act, guided by our intuition (inner knowing) from time to time.

Some of us who don't even believe in such things will admit to 'seeing' things or uncanny co-incidences. There are things 'beyond our ken' (knowing). As Shakespeare's Hamlet says, 'There are more things in heaven and earth (Horatio) than are dreamt of in your philosophy'.

Many of us are guided by our inner knowing, our dreams, hunches and inspiration. Great musicians, Mozart, Beethoven, amongst others, heard music in their heads and then wrote it down. Book themes, innovative creative ideas can be started by dreams and meditation ideas. After all, where do ideas come from? They can come from somewhere inside ourselves. Be willing to hear your inner guidance, be aware of your dreams. Make notes or keep a journal of these dreams and ideas and look for any trends or themes.

Take time out with meditation/prayer. Have some quiet time to listen to that inner soft-spoken gentle voice. 'Be still and know that I am God'. Let yourself be guided by your 'gut feelings', your Inner Knowing. There is a saying 'Prayer is when you talk to God. Meditation is when God/Spirit talks to you'.

You may hear your deceased loved one's voice guiding you or a sense of their presence.

Wishful thinking? Maybe yes and maybe no. Our loved ones essence is around us, trying to help and support us. They are around us to help us reach up and achieve our full potential.....

Have an 'Attitude of Gratitude'. Why?

By making note of the good things that have happened to you today, for the good things you have, a roof over your head, food in your tummy, loved ones and friends around. It is so easy to focus on the negative things in life.

Gratitude is essential. It aligns your thoughts with positivity and love. Things can seem less darkened; any sense of depression or limitation is lifted. List at least three things daily that you are grateful for. It could be about the simplest of things. Getting through a green traffic light, arriving to work on time, finding a parking space. Be thankful for your life, your health, your family and friends. By focusing on the positive, you bring more of that positivity into your life. The law of attraction, similar to affirmations. Your thoughts are energy and used positively can bring you benefits.

Make your home a sanctuary of peace and harmony. Bring nature indoors with houseplants, unless you are allergic.

Prayer can also uplift you. Try saying the Lord's Prayer or any prayer that touches you. The Serenity Prayer is used in 12-step programmes and I think it is a good one for all of us.

The Serenity Prayer

God grant me the Serenity to accept the things I can not change,
Courage to change the things I can
And the Wisdom to know the difference.

'Serenity is not freedom from the storm but
Peace amidst the storm'.

Chapter 12

Tools for Living Life Fully Now!

Why Are You Here?

Are you doing what you came here for and if not, why not?

Where did you get derailed – or who told you that, 'you could not'?

Not worthy, not good enough?

Are you being true to yourself?

Are You Doing It?

Are you living the life you truly want or do you have it on hold for when you grow up, when your children leave home, waiting until you retire?

We only have today. Make each day a day you want to record as an eventful day. Not necessarily being busy doing. It could be just Being… in the moment, during a walk or a talk on the bus or train.

Why Not?

What is your 'Yes but, If only'. All the excuses and deferrals are probably fear. Fear of the unknown, fear of failure or even fear of success.

Logic Is the Enemy!

It is good to have some ideas, plans and goals. But when they become the straightjacket, the excuse, the limitation rather than expansion, that is when it becomes the enemy. It stops spontaneity; it stops you hearing your inner voice and having the confidence to follow it, in spite of what others think or say or do. They are running on their fear, which is not always in your best interest. They fear change unless they are ready for it. Change in people they know and are close to can be scary because it might involve a change in them too.

How free are you daily in your approach to each day? How spontaneous are you moment to moment? Attend to your responsibilities. Have the ability to respond appropriately but don't hurt yourself or others. View each moment as if you only had today to be on this planet.

What If?

What if you live your life with a loose structure of plans and goals that are easily changeable if you should choose to?

How differently would you be and live? Where would you live, who with, doing what?

When you die, will you be able to say to yourself, 'I have achieved what I came here to do'? Whether it is to rear a child, gain money, help heal, teach or write. How have you helped to enrich this planet? It can be small; like creating a garden, drawing a piece of art, enriching someone's life as well as your own.

Start Today

Write a list of three things to do for the next day. Prioritise them. Start at number one. Complete it and then draw a line through it. It is very satisfying to draw that line as you have accomplished something and you are acknowledging that to your creative side. Then go to number 2, etc. Make a new list for tomorrow. You can have a small and large goal list.

Each night list three things that you are grateful for. Having an 'Attitude of Gratitude' brings more positive things into your life. Energy attracts similar energy.

Tell people often that you care and love them. Never assume they will always be there.

Spend 10–15 minutes daily meditating/reflecting, connecting with your inner self and spiritual aspect of yourself. It helps you feel more inner peace and contentment. Pray or talk to God or something greater outside yourself. Prayer can be a powerful energy. Prayer is when you talk to God and meditation is when God talks to you. Pray for yourself and your hopes and wishes; and for others' benefit.

Remember to have a balance between work and play… Do-Be-Do-Be-do!

We are human beings not human doings. Sitting and enjoying sitting is doing something.

Just say to yourself, 'I will not "should" on myself today!'

The trip of 100 miles starts with putting one foot in front of the other. Go with your gut instinct. If it feels right then it probably is. If it doesn't, then change the plan.

There are no failures. Just a path that you tried and found did not work for you, for now.

Be open to 'miracles' – little instances of guidance, occurrences, meetings and connections.

Keep your eyes open for opportunities. If a gate at airport security opens up and you are already in another (longer) line, what is to stop you from changing lane to get to the shorter quicker one? A survey was done which showed that very often the left lane moves more quickly! I ask the Angels/Spirits for car parking spaces. I let them know about a minute or two ahead of the need; where I want to park. After I get a parking space I thank them. I have to say this works 95% of the time, even in crowded areas.!

Don't settle for; dare to do.

Write down your dreams so that you remember them. Look over your dream journal every month and look for the common theme or story in your dreams. They can be your subconscious talking to you, guiding you if you choose to follow.

Make a date night regularly so you give real time to your loved one. Try to have a family meal at least once a week so you can really commune with your family with no electronics around!

If you have done wrong to someone, then apologise as soon as possible. Call them, write to them. If they are dead, you can still write a letter of apology to them; it will make you feel better.

If you argue with ones you love, please make up before you go to sleep.

If someone has wronged you, look at the part you played in the situation and see where you could have been different. If there was nothing you did that was wrong, then just forgive them and let it go.

Taking Care of You

Make sure you are prepared and that wills, advanced directives, funeral arrangements, etc., are current and relevant.

Be a blood donor to benefit others. It also makes your body produce some 'fresh' blood. Be willing to be a donor of your body or body parts and let loved ones know.

Keep your body healthy. Get regular blood pressure checks because high blood pressure has few if any signs and can lead to heart attacks, strokes and kill you. Regular bowel testing for hidden blood can also save lives. Ladies, please have regular breast checks and mammograms and cervical (Pap) smears. Gentlemen, please have your PSA blood tests for possible prostate problems. Early detection increases life survival.

Regular dental checks promote health. Teeth and gum infections can lead to bad breath and illness.

Life is about living and feeling; feelings are important and you will have highs and lows. My mother once said, 'It's facts that are important, not feelings'. I had to say I disagreed.

Life is a gift that we have been given and we should learn to enjoy the PRESENT, the NOW day by day. Be good to yourself, be good to others; respect your elders for their experiences and knowledge.

Be true to yourself, honour yourself and love yourself. This is not being selfish. Remember how you felt when you were in love with someone, the magic of each moment? Give that to yourself.

If each of us starts to live like this, imagine the harmony this planet would experience while you live your own heaven…on earth.

Dare to Be Different

Say to yourself, possibly into the mirror 'I am valuable, I am worthy, I have the right to be here'.

You not only have the right; you have the duty to yourself to find out who you are and why you have chosen to be here on this planet at this time? You never walk alone. You may feel alone at times but then you will meet up with like-minded people who will feel right to you. Their company will give you a sense of belonging, a sense of family, maybe even more than with your biological family.

'You cannot choose your family but you can choose your friends'.

Be prepared to view things differently, in more of an open way rather than a closed-minded one.

Be prepared for change as that is the only constant in life.

Walk through life with no regrets, if at all possible.

Allow more 'light' into your life. Light brings increased energy, colour, warmth, closer contact with spirit. Light lifts your spirit and makes you feel good. The old dark heavy stuff can be transformed into 'light', of weight, lightness and brightness.

De-clutter yourself of unnecessary possessions, gift them to others.

Become more aware, look around you and see how you can help others.

Look for the positive in the negative, the silver lining to the cloud, the ray of sunshine in the storm.

There is a belief that if you opt out of life you have to return again to re-learn the lesson.

For those of you thinking about suicide, please *talk* to others, professional or friends. Life is short enough anyway. You have much to give to others and things DO and WILL get better over time. You have no idea what possibilities are around the corner. Rest, talk and time will heal. Please don't leave and traumatise your loved ones forever. Their world would be emptier and not better without you. Think what great things you may do, create, achieve in time to come. You have been given the gift of life; please don't waste it.

Be in the Now, the Present and Observe the Mini Miracles

The available parking space, the unexpected meeting of old friends. Say thank you when these mini miracles happen. They are God's good instances, not just coincidences.

Give your life meaning. Don't just let yourself drift through life, thinking you will have time later.

If you can, do it now, for you do not know your given agenda of time. You may be fortunate and have many years and you may die tomorrow if your time on earth is done. Some of us die overnight with no warning. How sad it would be to find yourself 'gone' from here and thinking as you left that 'if only…' I meant to do that, I wish I had not wasted my time on earth.

The gift of life is just that, a gift. Do not waste it on drinking too much, drugging yourself or sitting around too much. Glory in the fact that you are alive and in a human body and look around you and see all the things you want to do or would like to do. Embrace life while you have the opportunity.

The ability to think, feel and be are glorious ones, and choices abound. So never dare say you are bored. If you are bored, it is because you are not living the life you want to live.

Do you smile when you meet someone? Are your eyes and heart smiling as well with the energy of love?

If not, how can you change that? What small steps can you do today that will make you feel better about yourself? You see this is all about you. You cannot change another. You can try to boss them around, control them, teach them, love them, but you can only truly change yourself. By changing how you are, others often change to adjust to the new you. Change can be frightening, but exciting as the new you emerges like a butterfly. Allow your wings to spread and let yourself fly, responsibly.

If you hurt others intentionally, emotionally, mentally or physically, in turn at some point you will need to ask for their forgiveness. The old saying 'What goes around comes around' or 'karma' is one of the lessons of life and balance.

Small steps start the process; you don't have to leap tall buildings. Have you always meant to buy yourself flowers, but felt it was an extravagance, that you did not deserve them? Or do you self-talk yourself into 'It's a waste of money just doing it for myself, I don't really need them'. It can be that small step each day that can bring huge changes into your life over time.

Drips of water over time can form stalagmites in limestone areas; can carve deep rivers,

What Can You Do for Yourself and for One Other Today?

It may just be a smile to a lonely looking person. That smile may seem nothing to you and costs you nothing, but it may make the difference to the other that would stop him/her jumping off a bridge.

You do not know your own power. Never put yourself down and never allow another to do so. They have their opinion, based on their perspective, their life experience. They do not know you fully and they do not know your path. Anyone who tries to put others down often don't feel good about themselves. They are not loving of themselves and want to lash out at others and blame others for their own unhappiness or discomfort with themselves.

Everyone wants to love and be loved. Imagine what this world could be like if we all started doing that. We can and it starts with self-love, not selfishness, but kindness to ourselves. If your own 'cup is full' it flows over and giving to others emotionally, energetically is easy, effortless. If we are 'drained' and tired, it is harder to give to others without resentment. So it is not selfish to take care of ourselves first. It allows us to nurture ourselves fully so that our 'cup runneth over' and then we can easily give love, encouragement and joy to others because we have plenty to spare. Not squeezing the last drop out of the drained empty cup, or holding back because our own cup is only half full and we then resent the giving.

Giving to ourselves first so that we can take care of others, can be as simple as buying yourself that bunch of flowers for no other reason than you want to. Not feeling guilty over it, but loving yourself enough to do it just for you, just because.... And then not beating yourself up for wasting money.

Just do it because you deserve it and it will do your soul/ spirit good. Let the action of self-love feed and nurture the essence of you. It will feed your soul. How else can you feed your soul?

Maybe many of us would not be so overweight if we fed our souls, and did some self-nurturing instead of stuffing food into ourselves to stop us from feeling empty, not hungry... empty.

Empty of love, full of self-loathing and trying to avoid the void by stuffing ourselves full to 'numb out' the empty feeling. Numbing out the self-loathing feelings with food to the extent that we stop feeling anything emotionally and feel bloated, full and fat. Which only then causes us to repeat the cycle and eat to stop feeling that self-loathing, that unhappiness, that lack of self-care and self-love. We blame others for judging us and our weight. Because we are hypersensitive to looks and comments and others think, they are helping us by making comments; but we are our own worst critics. The Western world admires slimness currently. It became fashionable to be thin during the depression of the 30s in America because so many people were starving and thin. Fashions change and nowadays Marilyn Monroe would be considered too fat. In other parts of the world, fat is admired because it equates with wealth. You have enough money to buy food to get fat on! Sometimes I wish I was living in those parts of the World!

If we fill ourselves up with contentment, self-worth, care and love, we will not need to fill ourselves up with overeating. Ask yourself why you are unhappy? Is it a new job you need?

It will probably not be the size-14 figure you are aiming for, because although it may give you satisfaction to reach your goal weight, it will not be 'enough' on some level.

The weight is an indicator of some need that is not being addressed. How can you change that underlying need? It is not a new boyfriend, new car, more money in the bank; those are material things, objects that represent the feelings of love, contentment, security. Once you 'get' those objects, the feeling in the moment will be great, but it will not last. If you can connect with the energy of the feeling that lies underneath the object, feed and satisfy that; then it will be enduring and more sustaining.

Ask yourself daily 'How can I nurture/care for myself and one other today'? If we all started doing that on a daily basis, imagine how the world could be different, full of souls taking care of themselves and others.

Balance is important in life. Do not over-work at the expense of your 'playtime'.

The acronym **ACE** is a good reminder: **A**chieve – chores, work study; **C**onnect – with family, friends; **E**njoy – pleasure, fun, play. Try to do some of ACE daily.

Start today, start now, in the present moment. Tomorrow you may not be around to make that difference. Make every minute count, even if it just getting under a blanket and reading to yourself for 15 minutes. That is time for self-nurture and feeding your soul.

You can self-talk judgment and criticism easily enough; just change it to a loving message instead.

Children are taught to discount positive comments and take on negative comments about themselves. In a European kindergarten, it was observed that many more comments from teachers to children were negative 'no, don't, stop, bad'.

Think how you will minimise a positive comment about yourself yet absorb the negative and focus on it. You could have nine people say thank you to you and you won't really take it in. Then one person is negative to you and you will think about it, believe it on some level and obsess over it for possibly hours. Allow yourself to accept the positive comments also. If someone 'wrongs you' and you feel like you have been attacked; check which part of you is upset.

Is it the adult in you or your inner child? Allow the tears and the hurt and the quivering chin for a few minutes. Feel the hurt so you can release it. Let the emotion pass through you. Then give yourself a hug. Reassure yourself and/or your inner child, the kid in you that hurts easily that it is OK and you will take care of him/her. Then forgive the offender. Realise they have their own agenda and mind play and that it may be personally directed to you; or you just happened to be the next face they saw and they were ready to lash out at someone. We do this usually to the people we feel safe with, our loved ones. That is no excuse though. Be big enough to let it go and move on. Use it as a learning tool and experience to grow by; resolve not to try to 'get back at that person' because you are stronger than that.

Adversity often strengthens us. I know a young man who was being bullied at school because he seemed different. He chose to not let it bother him. He was there for his reasons and did not need or seek the approval of others. The more they bullied him at school the stronger he got.

Be *that* convinced of your connection with spirit that no one can knock you off base. That does not mean you have to become arrogant and full of ego. It means to be so strong in your belief of yourself that you do not waiver from other peoples' opinions and viewpoints. Be open to their point of view because you might learn something. But remember that their point of view is just that, theirs; and they are entitled to that. What they think of you is not your business.

Dare to make a difference in your life.

Reach out with kindness to yourself, your inner child, your essence, your spirit, and one other person today. See the difference it makes to you, your day and your week. How it affects your circle of family, friends and co-workers.

By a smile, greeting, a pleasant sentence, you could change someone else's day too. See how it positively impacts your life.

Don't wait until tomorrow to live life to the full, do it today. So whether you die soon or when you are 100+, make sure you live well now.

'You cannot change the world,
but you can change Your World'!

Appendix A: Some Life-Threatening or Life-Limiting Conditions

Various types of cancers:

- Blood – Leukaemia, Hodgkin's Lymphoma, non-Hodgkin's Lymphoma
- Brain
- Mouth and Neck
- Breast
- Lung
- Oesophagus
- Stomach
- Liver and Pancreas
- Upper Colon
- Lower Bowel
- Kidney and Bladder
- Prostate
- Ovarian and Uterine
- Skin Melanoma

Other conditions:

- Heart conditions – Enlarged Heart, Heart Failure, Cardiac Arrhythmias
- Circulatory Conditions, including those associated with Diabetes
- Lung Conditions – Emphysema, Severe Asthma, Cystic Fibrosis, Chronic Obstructive Pulmonary Disease/COPD
- Neurological Conditions - Motor Neuron Disease/Lou Gehrig's Disease, Parkinson's Disease, Dementia including Alzheimer's Disease, Huntington's Disease
- Vascular Strokes
- Aneurysms of the Brain and Abdomen

Appendix B: Resources

Because this book is going to be printed internationally, I have deliberately not specified various forms of medical treatment because they vary from place to place.

Please be aware that your own doctors will guide your treatments. They are experts in their fields. Very often there are cancer boards or panels made up of doctors, surgeons, oncologists, and/or radiologists who consult together about your case and decide on the most appropriate treatment for you. If you feel strongly you cannot communicate with your doctor and that they are talking over you, then get another. It is important to have confidence in your medical practitioner.

Likewise, in each country there are different organisations and support systems for various types of illnesses. Your healthcare team can advise you what is available in your country. There are nursing care groups for cancer care, support groups and end-of-life care, whether you choose to die at home, in a hospice or hospital. In hospitals, there may be medical social workers who can assist you with information and resources.

For example, in the United Kingdom, there are organisations like MacMillan, Marie Curie, Maggie Centers, just to mention a few.

Maggie Centers. Places to go to talk, get support from staff and other patients. Also reading material for anyone with cancer and their families. These are located near hospitals, 14 currently with more planned in the future. Started by Maggie Keswick after a negative experience with how she was told she had cancer. Feeling she had no place to turn to, she started Maggie Centers.

Macmillan Cancer Support. Phone 0808-808-0000, www.macmillan.org.uk. Information and support. Nurses Advice Line during the week. Online chat room 24 hours a day.

Marie Curie Helpline. Phone 0800-090-2309, www.mariecurie.org.uk, Advice and support for terminal patients. Nurses take care of people in their last few days or weeks dying at home.

There are many books about cancer, palliative care available in bookstores and online.

This list is more about how you choose to live your life now:

'*Healing Words*' (The Power of Prayer/The Practice of Medicine), Larry Dossey, M.D.
'*Teach Only Love*' (Attitudinal Healing), Gerald G. Jampolsky, M.D.
'*Love, Medicine and Miracles*', Bernie Siegel, M.D.
'*The Power of Now*' and '*The New Earth*', Eckhart Tolle
'*Life after Life*', Raymond Moody, M.D., Near-Death Experiences.
'*Proof of Heaven*', Eben Alexander, M.D., Neurosurgeon's Near Death Experience.
'*Radical Remission*' by Kelly A Turner, PhD.
'*A Scottish Witch Doctor*' by Roger Melhuish.
'*A New Prescription for Addiction: A Comprehensive Treatment Plan*' by Richard L. Gracer, MD.

A Course in Miracles by Helen Schucman. Learning to live in love-based reality rather than fear-based reality. Books, courses and classes online.

Autobiography of a Yogi is an autobiography of Paramahansa Yogananda, a Yoga teacher from India who started Self-Realisation Fellowship in the United States of America in the 1920s. www.yogananda.org Worldwide organisation with courses and classes.

Index

O

P

Q

R